Table of Contents

Introduction

Environmental movements are an important part of the political and social spectrum today. The main principles developed by these movements are applied in politics, education, science nowadays. All we know about these principles. All we have encountered the conception that we need to keep nature clean, to protect the environment, etc. There is Paris agreement that aims at reducing greenhouse gases in the near future. There are other agreements demanding the elimination of fossil fuels. All the time we are listening about global warming, climate change, human impact on climate. We are informed that we will face natural disasters brought about by global warming; that all floods, storms, hurricanes in the near future will be caused by global warming. There is even a fashionable movement that we could refer to as "green." Everything "green" is good, nice, to be preferred. There are "green airlines," "green vehicles," "green factories," and so forth. This is what we hear and read, but is it true?

This book aims at analyzing environmental ("green") movements in a philosophical aspect. The work distinguishes between the political, scientific, and philosophical dimensions of these movements. It demonstrates that *here we can find a certain agenda elaborated and supported by liberal circles*. Despite that green movements do not have any connection to liberalism, they are backed by liberals today. Here we will attempt to answer the question of what is the relationship between environmental movements, liberalism, and socialism. Why do liberals support the global warming theory?

Although we will refer to a scientific problem such as global warming, we will not employ entirely scientific arguments. *This book is based on philosophical methods and understanding of the so-called global warming*. It is not a piece of research in the field of climatology, physics, chemistry, or biology. It is a philosophical analysis of a political problem that can be solved with references to contemporary science. Philosophy cannot do what climatology is able to do; but philosophy can check the validity of the arguments used in a debate. Through philosophy, we are able to understand the ongoing political, social, cultural processes that we can see nowadays.

Another important point to be discussed is the attitude of Green movements toward religion. In some sense, they establish a new religion. It is based on animism, paganism and pantheism. Therefore, the proponents of these movements are (1) liberals, (2) anti-capitalists, and (3) animists, that is, they denounce Christianity.

There are four chapters in the present work. The first chapter is focused on the history and main tenets of environmental movements. What are these movements? What are their goals? What are the factors facilitating their dissemination? There are many movements claiming to be "green." Which movement is really "green," and which is not? This chapter will show that environmental movements have a big influence on other political and social movements and doctrines.

The second chapter discusses the contemporary controversy over global warming. Global warming is a basic assumption of green movements. *They formulate it dogmatically and do not question it at all*. According to this dogma, decisions are made by politicians today. We will try to answer questions such as: Is there global warming? Is there a climate change? What is the human impact on the climate? Is there any effect of the measures against global warming? Additionally, we will analyze the United Nations agenda for sustainable development and the problem of "green energy". Is renewable energy enough to maintain our normal life? What will happen when we shut all our nuclear plants and reduce the use of fossil fuels?

The close links between environmentalists and socialism should be analyzed separately, which takes place in the third chapter. Green movements are not just about nature. They also profess ideas close to socialism. They believe that only a special type of socialism can protect nature. They think that capitalism destroys nature.

Here we will prove that capitalism (more precisely, marked-based economy) actually protects nature, and communist countries like China and North Korea destroy nature, just as it was during the Soviet era. We will give an example with Chernobyl and with current China's approach to nature. The so-called eco socialism will be subjected to our criticism.

The last chapter offers a Christian approach toward the environment. It criticizes the green movements for their atheist stance. Green movements are diverse. Still, some of their members tend to take ideas from paganism, animism, and pantheism. Here we will consider their attitude towards Christianity and show that there is no way for a true Christian to adhere fully to the principles of the green movements. Nonetheless, a Christian believer can protect nature and be actively involved in this protection. Christianity claims that man has to love nature as he loves God and himself.

Preserving nature is our common duty, but from the point of view that God created it and he makes us responsible for its use. The earth and nature should not become gods that we worship. The world is our temporary home, and we need to take care of it; but it is not our only home. We will prove that we should love our planet because it is also inhabited by many other living beings. They were created by God with good intentions.

As we noted, the current work is not of scientific importance. However, it attempts to analyze contemporary environmental movements and to reveal the truth about their popularity and why they are supported by our liberals. We will demonstrate that some of the theories and ideas promoted by the green movements are not rooted in any scientific fact and that such movements turn out to be a new ideology.

Chapter I: History and core ideas of environmental movements

To understand exactly what environmental movements want, we must first look at their history. And this story is also about understanding nature. Here we will look at various issues such as the concept of nature, the emergence and development of environmental movements, and their *politicization* in the 20th century. Only a small part of the history of environmental movements will be discussed here.

1.1. History of environmentalism

Summary:

The concepts of nature and environmentalism will be defined here. Our understanding of nature has not been the same all the time. The history of environmental movements will be outlined in short. Contemporary environmentalism will be shown to be different from its forms in the 18th and 19th centuries.

This subchapter will start our analysis with the understanding of the concept of nature. Then we will turn to the emergence of the environmental movements in the 18th century. An interesting philosopher, Henry David Thoreau, will be discussed with his ideas on nature and idealism. Finally, we will show what distinguishes the movements in the 20th centuries from their predecessors.

1.1.1 What is "nature"?

To understand what environmental movements want, we must first analyze the concept of "nature." Speaking of nature, environmentalists adhere to the traditional division of the world into "nature" and "culture". Nature is everything that does not depend on man; culture is everything that man can produce or create. This traditional dichotomy has existed for several centuries, since the beginning of the modern era (17th-18th century). And we still perceive of it as real: we think that nature is completely different from culture.

Today, nature is defined as everything material that is around us and is not produced by man. Nature are grasses, flowers, trees; but nature is the stars and the planets (including the sun); and finally, nature is all the natural laws that govern our world. As we can see, the concept of "nature" is very broad. Many of us grasp it in an intuitive manner: we know what is nature although we cannot define it. As the philosopher Jose Augusto Padua remarks, "Since Antiquity, nature has always been a central category of human thought, at least in Western culture" (Padua 83).

His article is focused on the concept of nature in Greece. In Ancient Greece, "nature" was a notion associated with something essential to all things. The most important human qualities were called "nature". Man was considered an integral part of the world, which is why he was seen as part of nature. Later, the Stoics[1] introduced the concept of nature as a universal law. The *Logos*, according to the Stoics, is what rules the whole world; all people and immaterial things obey it. To the Stoics, nature is reason, and

---

[1] The school of Stoics had two main branches: one in Greece and in one Rome. Initially, they were founded as a philosophical school dealing with problems related to logic. Later, after the expansion of the Empire founded by Alexander the Great, Stoicism became popular in Rome. The form of Stoicism taught in Rome was ethical. Philosophers such as Seneca dealt with moral issues: what is the meaning of life; what is death; what is immortality; what is suffering. Stoicism is famous for its moral doctrine, but its logic and epistemology should not be omitted from view.

reason is nature. Thus, they came to the conclusion that *everything taking place in our life is rational and necessary*. They did not see any real difference between nature and culture.

But other philosophers such as Aristotle pointed out that nature is everything internal or inborn. As Padua explains it, "Natural things would be those things that exist by themselves, in the sense of possessing in themselves the principle of their movement and rest" (Padua 86). As Padua puts stress on another idea developed by the great Greek thinker, "When human observers contemplate the reality of existence, they realize that the overwhelming majority of things that exist, including the fundamentals of the material edifice that enables their existence, are not human creations" (Padua 86).

This was related to Aristotle's conception of the Prime Mover, or God: after God made the initial movement, then all existing things began moving by themselves. However, they owe their existence to God; and God is the only real entity that exists by itself entirely and unconditionally.[2] Therefore, nature is somehow associated with the movement of all things, at least in Aristotle's philosophy.

With the end of Ancient Greece and Rome (about 4th century AD), their conception of the integrity of man and nature was exhausted. Then Christianity became more popular and God was seen as the Creator and the One Who really exists. Nothing and no one else exist for real.

During the Middle Ages, philosophy was based entirely on Christianity. It perceives the whole world as nature. Why is the world nature? Because everything is created by God, therefore it is "nature". In that case, man is also "nature." Therefore,

---

[2] This form of teaching of God is called *deism*. It was employed by the French philosopher Rene Descartes later.

even then, “nature” meant rather something related to the way things exist. Things are as they are; they cannot be others. This is their nature. However, man is seen as something different from animals and all other creatures. Man is the “crown of creation.”

It is true that Christian philosophy, as we will see in the last chapter of the present work, also comprehends man as a part of nature. But its conception of nature is different from the Ancient or the modern one. Nature is simply the world of creation. This means, God is not nature, and angels are not nature.

In the modern era the concept of nature was redefined. Then the dichotomy between man and nature appeared again. Philosophers of modernity (Immanuel Kant, Georg Hegel, John Locke) believed that man is completely different from nature. The problem of nature was seen in its relation to civil society and the state. Jean-Jacques Rousseau, for example, believed that life in the “civilization” is very different from that in the “state of nature.” The latter is a state of peace, tranquility and understanding between people. Rousseau criticized the political system of European monarchies and thought that moving back to nature would be beneficial to the people.

Rousseau was influenced by romanticism, a movement in art and literature that perceives nature as something magical and beautiful, unlike man-made objects. As Jose Padua observes, this dichotomy can be seen easily today: “The human image and the image of human history were built largely by opposition to nature: art versus nature, social order versus nature; technique versus nature; spirit versus nature etc” (Padua 87).

To all this, we can add the opposition between natural science and humanities and arts; Physics, Biology and Chemistry are often called science, not Philosophy or

Psychology. This is also due to our understanding that man and nature are separate entities.

Today we can see this romantic admiration for nature in the supporters of the green movement. They see nature as something perfect that can only be imitated. We should not criticize how nature works. It has a higher level of organization than we as individuals. The collective is considered by these people to be more than the individual. Our individual existence as human beings is often permeated by mistakes and weaknesses. On the other hand, nature is not wrong - it is always right. We are the ones that must refrain from any action against nature.

The Greens' view of the earth, for example, is similar. Our planet is perceived as a perfect organism that does not need our help. It existed before us and will exist after our extinction as a species. The earth is not just a planet, it is not just a collection of inanimate matter; it is a system whose "organs" are the seas, forests, continents, atmosphere, animals, and humans. Any interference in one of these "organs" will lead to problems for this perfect system. This understanding is rooted in the views of the 18th and 19th century Romantics and their conception that everything that exists is alive and that "inanimate matter" has a special form of consciousness.

All this does not mean that the concept of nature is socially constructed or a matter of cultural differences. It merely means that nature can be seen from different perspectives. Nature is always nature, and it cannot be called in a different way; but the most important question is the place of man in nature. Environmental movements base their understanding on the modern conception of man and his relation to nature.

Nowadays, nature is seen more in terms of collective entities. It is understood as a system standing above all of its constituents. As Padua notes, "The natural sciences have achieved greater theoretical sophistication, basing themselves on radically open and interactive ecological methods. Natural systems are now seen as self-organizing through the constant interaction between all its elements" (Padua 90). These elements, as he remarks are biotic (humans, animals, plants) and abiotic (stones, oceans). This attitude is seen in the view of environmentalism, namely that our planet is a system that cannot be defined by any of its parts taken separately. This view is usually contrasted to the mechanical view of the earth as the place in which various material entities are located. This idea was widespread by the end of the 19th century.

The view of the earth as a systematic whole is also based on the advancement of science and the emergence of new technologies. It is believed that contemporary technologies seem to be a system, and not a mere mechanism. Scientists and engineers consider contemporary machines as well-integrated collectives; one of the best examples of this view is the computer. A computer is a system that can work only when all of its parts interact properly, according to a certain program. Of course, computers are produced by human beings, thus we cannot compare them to the earth entirely. But the fact is that computers help us understand nature better. Jose Padua observes the following: "In the advanced industrial world…new technologies penetrate the processes of nature in ways that were unthinkable in the past… A perception of the living unity between natural systems and human beings is becoming increasingly necessary" (Padua 94). In brief, there is a new relationship between man and the machine, and we need to take it as changing our attitude toward nature. For, what is a machine: a living being or an inanimate thing?

All this means that the mechanical view of nature, which was popular in the 17th and 18th centuries, is now replaced by a view, which we could call synergetic. It is not simply a view but rather an approach toward everything material. This approach is based on the assumption that all material things are part of particular systems and they can only be defined in terms of systems and interaction. In this sense, it is not important whether nature is alive or not; what only matters is that it exists in unity, in harmony, and all of its parts are necessary constituents of this system. Animals, humans, plants, stones, waters, air, cannot be separated from each other because they exist in unity in the system called earth. Therefore, humans need to realize that their actions can influence the work and efficiency of this system. Human impact is visible and real by definition; the very existence of human beings means that they are interconnected with other parts of this integral system. This is the fundamental idea of all environmental movements.

1.1.2 Emergence of environmental movements

Let's start our analysis of environmental movements with a few essential definitions. *An environmental movement is a political or social movement that is based on the principle that nature and its resources must be protected through strict control.* Otherwise, according to the supporters of this movement, there would be natural disasters in the future - pollution of the atmosphere, water and soil, or melting ice at the North

Pole, which in turn will lead to massive floods throughout the world. So the idea of a natural disaster is paramount to green movements.

In order to achieve their goals, environmental movements require the intervention of states both individually and internationally. Policies to protect nature and natural resources must be put in place and the hypothetical damage caused by people must be reduced. All this cannot be done by the citizens alone, because they do not have the capacity to do so. In addition, green policies must be enforced because part of the world's population does not have the necessary awareness and knowledge about future environmental disasters.

Thus, we understand that the green movements are striving to achieve something that, in their words, will save us from an ecological disaster. In turn, they offer various scientific arguments in favor of their ideas, but some of them are too broad in perspective and difficult to verify. For example, a future environmental catastrophe that has not yet begun cannot be verified. Their beliefs are rather beliefs that are difficult to verify. We will show this further.

Another typical feature of these movements is the principle of globalism. They believe that *global action must be taken to prevent a future environmental cataclysm.* These actions must be organized and controlled at a supranational level, for which special institutions need to be set up. Later in this book, we will see that some green supporters oppose globalization because they see it as a major factor in the over-industrialization of the planet. This is a clear paradox that is difficult to explain.

We will talk about these principles later. Now is the time to look at the beginning of environmental movements. It should be mentioned here that we focus entirely on the history of Western civilization, although in China and India there were similar ideas[3] to those of environmental movements. In any case, industrialization was a major factor in the development of these movements. That is why we believe that they appeared most clearly within Western civilization.

In one of his articles, the researcher Robert Falkner discusses the history of environmentalism, especially as regards international relations. He claims that the origin of green movements can be traced back to romanticism, but the industrial revolutions were the trigger for its systematic development. He pays heed to the opposition between romanticism and industrialization and observes the following: "As the industrial revolution spread from England to continental Europe and North America, naturalist writers and Romantic poets turned the aesthetic appreciation of nature into a concern for nature's integrity and survival" (Falkner 511-512).

The idea that we must protect nature and its resources clearly emerged in the second half of the 18th century. It was developed mainly in France and America. In France, it had some connection with liberalism, which was trying to impose a new political organization on the state. Jean-Jacques Rousseau emphasized that all people are equal by birth, no matter what their economic status. It was a step backwards toward nature, which shows that the whole existing structure of society is a matter of convention, not of nature. Inequality is thus a matter of human (social) convention, i.e. of norms that were formulated by certain people for their own benefit.

---

[3] Jainism in India is a religion claiming that we should love and respect every living being. All animated beings feel pain when we hurt them, therefore we should not do any harm to them- even to insects. This teaching has been accepted by the green movements and taken as their core element. A similar doctrine can be found in Tibetan Buddhism. In China, one can search for "environmentalist" elements in Taoism, but this religion cannot be considered "environmentalist."

One of the first more profound theories, which we can call environmentalist, appeared in the works of American writer and philosopher Henry David Thoreau. He was one of the leading representatives of the so-called transcendentalist movement in the United States. His theory can be seen in various of his essays and literary works such as *Walden*. He insists that man is part of nature and must live in harmony with it. Nature stands above man and we should not place ourselves above it; we should not try to control it because it is governed by its laws and not by our laws.

Jason Matzke, a researcher of Thoreau's work, puts emphasis on the fact that for Thoreau man is connected in two ways to nature: "In addition to our physical participation in, and dependence upon, our environment, we are connected to nature spiritually. Thoreau claims that we humans are both 'earth born' and 'heaven born'" (Matzke 172). Thoreau, like his fellow Ralph Waldo Emerson, was an idealist and claimed that the primary substance of the world is ideal, or spiritual. In spite of being influenced by Hegel's objective idealism, Thoreau did not claim that nature itself is God. In such a sense, he was not precisely a pantheist. This is remarked by Matzke who points out that "We can note at least that nature is not itself God (or ultimate Mind or Spirit) or the body of God since, for example, within a single sentence Thoreau calls nature our mother and God our father" (Matzke 173).

The idealism of this American philosopher is not purely metaphysical, unlike Ralph Emerson's idealism. It is rather based on his moral convictions. In a sense, this appeal to nature has an aesthetic dimension. Nature is beautiful; we feel pleasure when we observe it and when we see that we are part of it. Therefore, we can say that Thoreau is an ethical and aesthetic idealist rather than a metaphysical one. As Matzke confirms, "being not merely physical ourselves, we can at times experience some of the ineffable spiritual reality beyond our narrow selves" (Matzke 173).

To understand all this, we need to take a look at German idealism of the 18th century. The opposition man-nature is clearly seen in the works of three of its greatest representatives, Johann Fichte, Friedrich Schlegel and Georg Hegel. For all of them, the Absolute Spirit, or Mind, or Idea, stands at the beginning of creation. But Fichte was the first to define nature as non-self. Thus, man is not nature because man is a Self; and everyone is a personality. Nature, on the contrary, is impersonal, faceless; it does not have any unique "face."

Schlegel and Hegel moved this conception further: the history of the world is a process, a development from the Absolute Idea. This history passes through three stages: spiritual (the reality of the Absolute Idea and the Act of Creation), material (when nature appears with all its natural laws), and human (which is a synthesis of spiritual and material). For all of them, man and nature exist in unity, but it is a dialectical unity- there is a struggle between them, and at the same time, man and nature coexist in harmony. This principle was developed further by Georg Hegel whose system of objective idealism is probably the most complete metaphysical system ever elaborated.

This type of idealism is not dualism, at least in the sense offered by Rene Descartes in the 17th century. It is also not pantheism, since pantheists reject the reality of God. Pantheistic is, for example, Hinduism, with its emphasis on the identity of the Universal Soul with the individual soul, or man. Pantheism claims that all nature is divine and that nothing stands above it. It does not say who created nature. Maybe nature just appeared on its own? But Hegel's philosophical system is not pantheism[4]; this means that Thoreau and Emerson, who are influenced by him, are not pantheists.

Matzke notes that the colleague and friend of Thoreau, Ralph Waldo Emerson, "seems to waver between a Berkeley-like idealism and a dualism where the significance of the material is secondary to the spiritual" (Matzke 174). George Berkeley is famous for his subjective idealism, claiming that only what is in perception is real. Dualism of Cartesian type (as proposed by Descartes) is also an option here. At any rate, both Thoreau and Emerson do not see nature as divine in itself, but rather as penetrated by something divine, by spiritual substance.

All this does not lead to the conclusion that our needs and interests are identical with those of nature. We cannot exist in perfect harmony with nature, even though this is the ideal possible state. Matzke asks the question: Why does Thoreau sometimes contrasts human interests to nature? And he answers in the following manner: "Even as a part of nature, we naturally have interests that conflict with those of other entities" (Matzke 175-6). Or, man and nature exist in opposition.

This assertion can be interpreted as follows: man is part of nature, but he also has ambitions and aspirations leading him beyond nature. Our desire to conquer, to develop, to build, opposes nature. We need buildings to live in; we need cities to organize ourselves in society. Therefore, we have to conquer territories from animals; we have to cut trees; and we have to cultivate plants and domesticate animals. In such a way, Thoreau demonstrates that some human needs oppose the state of nature.

---

[4] Hegel's philosophical system is usually called Absolute idealism.

Thoreau offers a criticism of our civilization. Matzke explains that "life immersed in civilization restricts an individual's opportunities to grow as a person. Society has both a conforming and a limiting influence on its members" (Matzke 177). We are social animals, as Aristotle says, and we need to live together with other persons. But society puts limitations on our ambition and needs. We must follow certain rules that are a result of a convention. Civilization itself is good but it has some shortcomings. We have to take into account the fact that it does not allow for our personality to grow and evolve in full. Whether school or job or another institution, we are forced to restrict our own actions and beliefs, because some of them could do harm to society as a whole. In school, we have to sit and attend our classes carefully. We are eager to have good marks because they will help us achieve more- to find a better job and to have a better education.

According to the interpretation of Matzke, "Greed leads people to cut down trees, ignoring their higher uses, and to take the world around them for granted" (Matzke 178). Here we can see the potential conflict between humans and nature: humans want to control nature and to define the rules of the game. Nature does not agree and is ready to resist in any possible respect. Whether greed or another ambition leads us, we "invade" more areas belonging to nature, and we hope that nature will respond positively to our actions.

Nature always finds a way to restore balance. And yet, Thoreau does not predict anything disastrous. Probably in the early 19th century, it was difficult to imagine anything like global warming or another natural disaster. Thus, it turns out that Thoreau's conception is more like a critique of the modern way of life than a doctrine of environmental protection. His idealization of nature is seen in another passage interpreting Thoreau's thought about nature: "Life in communion with nature provides the needed redemption. Lives of desperation become free and peaceful as higher law is recognized… Nature helps us identify and understand higher law" (Matzke 178).

Here we see that for Thoreau, our life must be subordinated to something higher than what our senses and thoughts give us. This thing is of a spiritual nature and is called a "higher law." If we live against this law, we will only suffer and be in despair. If we live in harmony with nature, will we be able to live according to this law.

Matzke concludes his analysis by emphasizing that "what is needed is the wildness of nature. This wildness (not necessarily wilderness) frees us from the confining effects of society and thereby allows us to think more simply and clearly" (Matzke 179). To some extent, we are "wild," which means that we can exist outside of any norms and obligations. Here we can see a way of thinking that precedes the evolutionary theory of Charles Darwin. Although Thoreau wrote his essays about nature before the publication of the work of Darwin, we can notice some similar features there. However, Darwin's work is based on the materialist worldview and the idea that man is an animal, although an animal of a higher type.

This romantic vision of the human-nature relationship to some extent influences modern environmental movements. Here, however, there is one difference - Thoreau was not affected by the sudden progress of industrialization, which in the first half of the 19th century was at a fairly low level. The environmentalism of 20th century is the logical outcome of strong and intensive industrialization, contamination and pollution of the environment. However, Thoreau was aware that the destruction of environment will have negative impact on mankind.

Focusing on environmental issues is not entirely new to humanity. There may be cases where there is talk of the need to protect nature. But it was not until the 19th century that there was a systematic talk about natural resources and the need to protect the environment. As the Brazilian researcher Padua remarks, "Historical research has revealed that, at least in the world of European extraction, intellectual concern with 'environmental' problems has existed since the late 18th century and played an important role in the construction of modern thought" (Padua 82). It has something to do with modernity because modern times are the age of industrialization. The philosophy of modernity has tried to explain both industrialization and technologies with their impact on our life. Nonetheless, the greatest philosophers of modernity, among them being Rene Descartes, John Locke, Immanuel Kant, Georg Hegel, never paid heed to the problem of conservation of nature. For them, metaphysics was much more important as an answer to the question, what is the world and how it appeared?

As Padua notes, the first book focused entirely on environmental issues was *Man and Nature or Physical Geography Modified by Human Action*. It was written by the diplomat George Marsh in 1864. Padua comments that "This work, although heavily focused on the European and Mediterranean context, sought to review the changes wrought by human action since Antiquity on the flora, fauna, forests, waters and sands, having as main vector the denouncement of destruction" (Padua 84-5). Marsh was probably the first to emphasize that we need to keep our resources and control them properly. His study relied on historical data as well as his own impressions from the journeys across Europe (he was an ambassador to the Ottoman Empire and Italy). The researcher J. R. MacNeill observes that "Marsh argued… that human action, mainly farming, degraded environments to the point where agricultural production was threatened." He adds that "His evidence came mainly from his native Vermont and his travels in Italy and the Ottoman Empire, where he held diplomatic posts. Marsh came into vogue again in the 1960s, at least in scholarly circles" (McNeill 15). That is, Marsh was studied in the middle of the 20th century with regards to his views on the environment.

To be sure, the interest in environmental problems has had a direct bearing on the emergence of evolutionary theory. Since man is nothing more than an animal (as Darwin claims), evolutionism concludes that man will disappear one day. The course of evolution logically predetermines that there will be a day when all people on earth will have disappeared. Therefore, this is a potential danger that needs to be talked about. If mankind disappears, what will follow then? Will another human race appear?

On the other hand, the biblical explanation of the creation of the world has been criticized by Darwin and his colleagues. This led to serious confusion among 19th-century philosophers and intellectuals. As Padua notes, "Biblical chronology (at least as interpreted in the ecclesiastical milieu) began to undergo severe shocks in the 18th century." For instance, "The French naturalist Buffon was able to imagine that Earth existed 'some 70 thousand years' before the appearance of man. A little later, in the early 19th century, geologists were already conceiving the planet on a scale of millions, not thousands, of years" (Padua 87). This observation can easily explain why contemporary environmentalists are both evolutionists and (mainly) atheists. Gradually, the view of the alleged decline and even disappearance of mankind took place. This view was probably taken by the Greens. But there was much more to talk about in the field of ecology.

1.1.3 Contemporary environmentalism

Contemporary environmental movements have been developed in response to rapid industrialization, deforestation, and urbanization. Unlike those preceding them, they look more professional, with persons engaged in organizing environmentalist campaigns all year round. These movements have their share in academia, in schools, and even in political parties. Their ideas have influenced the business and now something like "green business" is appearing.

Some worries related to pollution and contamination were expressed as early as in the 1880s and 1890s. This took place particularly in America with its large cities and multitude of factories. America was seen as the land of freedom then, and plenty of immigrants came to the United States at the turn of the century. America needed a workforce, and this workforce needed to have a good job. New factories and even new industries appeared then. New York, Chicago, Detroit, and London were probably the most industrialized cities in the world at that time.

The first ecological movements emerged as groups for conservation of parks and forests. Their aim was to limit the process of deforestation and to emphasize the need to protect nature. Many countries acted domestically, without coordination with their neighbors. However, environmentalism became an international movement with the First congress for the protection of nature in Paris (1909).

In 1913 another event was held of international character, but it was interrupted by the First World War. The interwar years were a period of economic restoration, so no one was eager to put emphasis on the protection of nature. The actual international movement in the field of environmentalism emerged after the Second World War.

The researcher Robert Falkner puts emphasis on the problem of international cooperation in the field of environmentalism. According to him, international action was hard to achieve in the first decades of the 20th century. For example, "Nineteenth-century conservationism addressed some of the first transnational environmental concerns of the time, but remained a predominantly national movement in outlook and organization. It had little impact on international relations" (Falkner 512). Another thing is that every country has its own approach and its own issues. Some countries have a deficit of water; other countries feel worried regarding potential floods; other countries suffer from drought; and so forth. This is why it is hard to implement international cooperation.

However, as Falkner claims, there can be some common elements found in the environmental programs of every country in the world: "Environmentalism, like other political ideologies, is a broad church based on a wide range of ethical and political beliefs. It seeks to rebalance the relationship between human society and the natural environment" (Falkner 511). We already noted this diversity among environmentalists: they adhere to various ideas, but still there are a few main ideas that are shared by all green activists.

According to Falkner, *the birth of contemporary environmentalism is to be found in international cooperation*. Therefore, *this new type of environmentalism is distinguished by its international character*; that is, countries try to solve ecological issues together, not separately. International NGOs emerged that seek some solutions to such problems. At the UN level state actors also are very active and try to launch and realize programs that will reduce greenhouse emissions. We need to note the role of globalization in this process- without globalization, the current state of international cooperation would have been very unclear. We will discuss the globalist dimension of environmentalism later.

As Falkner remarks, the first United Nations conference on the environment was held in 1972, but it was boycotted by some Communist states. It was followed by the Stockholm declaration. With the fall of Communism, international cooperation became visible in all regions of the world, and now former Communist states actively cooperated with their former "enemies." There was a summit in Rio de Janeiro, Brazil, described by Falkner as follows: "Helped by the end of the Cold War and a renewed effort to accommodate developing countries' concerns, the Rio 'Earth Summit' of 1992 attracted near-universal participation and support" (Falkner 513).

At the beginning of the 21st century, the so-called Millennium Development Goals were developed by the United Nations (2000). One of these goals was related to protection of the environment and the resources on earth (Goal 7). We will discuss them further, but we can say here that *contemporary environmentalism is systematic and coherent; it is implemented in all possible spheres of life and human activity.*

Modern environmentalism is of international and/or global character. A perfect example of the development of environmentalism is the history of Greenpeace. This organization was founded in 1971 when several American and Canadian green activists protested against the planned detonation of nuclear weapons in Alaska. Their direct action was illegal, but it attracted the attention of other activists in North America. In 1979 an international Greenpeace organization was founded with thousands of members around the world. They spread around the world and established local branches in plenty of countries.

Today their actions are more of propaganda type, i.e. they rarely attack power plants or fishing ships. On their web page we can read the statement regarding their mission: "Greenpeace is a global, independent campaigning organization that uses peaceful protest and creative communication to expose global environmental problems and promote solutions that are essential to a green and peaceful future" (Greenpeace). This means, they stopped using violence and are now prone to peaceful campaigns and action.

Among their particular goals we can find the following: "Greenpeace has indeed changed the world. And we continue to make the world a better place. Our committed activists and supporters have come together to ban commercial whaling, convince the world's leaders to stop nuclear testing, protect Antarctica" (Greenpeace). Here we see the idea that all green activists from the whole world need to be united and to act together.

The actions of Greenpeace have inspired plenty of small local NGOs to work in the field of environment protection. Contrary to their reception in the 1970s and 1980s, Greenpeace is now a highly respected and wide-known organization. But this only demonstrates how strong has been the influence of environmental organizations and their lobbies on policy-makers and business owners.

One could think that all this is a matter of a secret agreement between politicians, business companies, academia, and environmentalists. In all cases, we are witnessing the constant and ubiquitous propagation of the core ideas of environmentalism. What about these ideas? Now we will discuss them in short.

1.2 Core ideas of environmentalism

Summary:

Here the main tenets and core ideas of environmental movements will be presented and analyzed critically. We will discuss 7 core ideas that are common to all green organizations.

Now is the time to move on to the fundamental beliefs and convictions of environmental movements. It should be noted that *despite their diversity, these movements share similar principles*. This fact is rooted in globalization and the idea of international cooperation. As Robert Falkner points out, "What the different environmental traditions have in common are two core convictions: an empirical belief that many of the planet's ecosystems and species are under threat, and a normative belief that humans should take greater care of the environment" (Falkner 511). As we see, personal convictions are connected with moral principles. According to Falkner's interpretation, ethics is an essential part of green activism.

The core ideas of environmental movements are partly based on science, but they nevertheless spread as "scientific facts" that cannot be denied. Thus, many people are deluded that the personal beliefs of the participants in the green movements are entirely scientific and that they are entirely true, without any distortion due to their personal bias and desires. We will look at the theory of global warming, for example, and see that it is not entirely based on science, at least because it is difficult to verify. Likewise evolutionary theory, *global warming theory spans an extended period of time that cannot be verified by personal observation.* Therefore, this theory relies only on indirect evidence.

Here are the core principles of environmental movements, to which we will add some comments:

1. Human activity directly and visibly affects nature and the environment in a negative context. Man harms nature by polluting the air, water and soil. In addition, man cuts down forests, hunts endangered species, and causes irreparable damage to the environment.

Comment: This is an idea that cannot be disputed. We all agree that human activity leads to certain harms. Air pollution is so obvious that no one would deny it. This is a fact in the largest cities in the world both in summer and in winter. The link between human activity and given environmental disasters has been proven. Whether the oil spill in the Gulf of Mexico or the Chernobyl accident, but everything shows that people are not nature's best friend. Of course, there are countries that pollute more than others; this is exactly what we will talk about in this book.

2. Rapid and adequate measures must be taken, otherwise the situation will become irreparable. This means that every little delay is leading to a global environmental catastrophe. It can still be prevented, but it depends on our desire and ability.

In the 19th century there was a strong tendency to preserve forests and create nature reserves. Unlike then, green movements claim that the process is global and inevitable. We must act quickly to stop this supposed catastrophe.

Our comment is as follows: The concept of quick action is irrational. People must act on the basis of knowledge. One should not act impulsively, based on fear and anxiety. Our actions must correspond to reality. In the past, for example, there have been many natural disasters. The presumed extinction of dinosaurs is a similar example, showing that the extinction of species (if there is such a process at all) is not due to humans alone. Furthermore, it has been suggested that there were high levels of carbon dioxide in the atmosphere in the past, so raising these levels today may not be related to human activity. In any case, the alarmism of environmental movements should not be taken blindly.

3. There is global warming, or at best climate change. These processes are directly related to human activity - for example, to the industry as well as transportion. That is why we need to reduce greenhouse gases and fossil fuels. Otherwise, serious warming and floods are ahead.

Comment: Global warming is considered an absolute dogma of environmental movements, although recently there has been a lot of talk about climate change, i.e. this warming is not constant. This dogma is the basis of many economic policies that we see carried out at the moment at the international level. It is the basis of various agreements to reduce greenhouse gas emissions.

4. Reducing greenhouse gas emissions requires a shift to a new type of energy. This is the so-called green energy, which is produced from renewable sources. The goal is (1) to reduce the use of fossil fuels, and (2) to use sources that are openly available - water, wind, biomass, solar energy. These sources are considered to be inexhaustible, unlike fossil fuels.

Comment: Green energy is a great idea, but it is not clear who is behind the planning of its use. There is the so-called green business that deals only with the production of green energy or its infrastructure. It should be mentioned that green companies receive significant financial subsidies. On the one hand, this is in order to motivate energy producers to switch to green energy. On the other hand, it is discrimination that imposes dictates on the energy market. Traditional energy producers are not competitive and at some point will have to give up. It remains doubtful if government intervention here will help some companies and others. This is not fair, and it is not clear whether it will have a positive effect.

We will later analyze the case in Texas in the winter of 2021, when it turned out that green energy was not enough to power all of Texas.

5. A sustainable economy must be created that uses few resources but in an efficient way. This must be an economy based not on growth and profit, but on **sustainability**.

Comment: The idea of sustainability is pretty common in various spheres of human activity today. Sustainability means the ability for a system to handle itself on its own and with little external resources. However, is it possible for our economy to be sustainable in this sense? This idea has met with much criticism.

For instance, Robert Falkner says that the ideas of the environmentalists (to which we can add this one) are "in direct tension with the principles of market-based capitalism. The modern environmental movement of the 1960s and 1970s, in particular, identified the industrial and expansionist logic of capitalism as a root cause of the global ecological crisis" (Falkner 520). But this attitude of the green activists is wrong and inadequate.

The problem with the sustainable economy is that it is based on a strong state control. Therefore, the principle of the free market is violated, which will eventually lead to collapse - because any form of communism ends in economic catastrophe. Furthermore, we are not sure exactly how a sustainable economy works. What will we have to abandon? What should we limit? Do we need to change our lifestyle and why? Is it all worth it?

6. We can tackle environmental challenges only together and through international cooperation. This means that all countries in the world must contribute to the protection of the environment and to the achievement of the points listed so far. This is what Robert Falkner calls "global environmentalism". As he says, it "has had a lasting, and potentially transformative, impact on international relations. Over the last hundred years, international society has slowly but steadily been 'greened', despite many setbacks in the search for practical solutions "(Falkner 503).

Comment: This international cooperation has become *an attempt to impose certain norms based on the ideas of green movements*. Falkner observes that "Given its potential to alter the social structure of international relations, the rise of global environmental responsibility deserves to be recognized as a major example of the normative expansion of international society" (Falkner 504). Here we clearly see the connection between green movements and the changes in the legislative aspect at the national and international levels. They seek total control over the legislation, adding ethical issues. But this environmental responsibility is not based on objective legal criteria. It is a matter of subjectivity, therefore it should not be applied to legislation.

7. One way to achieve these goals is through universal education about ecology and sustainable development. In short, this is the idea of integrating different approaches and practices from various areas. Environmental problems are solved in various fields such as economics, politics, science and technology, education. These areas cannot have their own approach to these problems, because this will only lead to partial solutions.

Comment: What is more important here is that green movements are trying to impose their views globally, regardless of location and specific culture or geographical location. They operate both locally and globally. Their ideas have been accepted by politicians, political parties and international organizations. In addition, they want to impose the idea that environmental education helps open borders to people and goods - in short, Greens are defending globalization! *Green movements adhere to multiculturalism, tolerance of foreign cultures and religions*, and oppose the closure of state borders. They argue that multiculturalism protects the environment and that conservatism harms nature.

To better understand these movements, we must recall that they criticize the national state. According to them, we must protect nature and natural resources together, and individual countries act selfishly. This hinders the achievement of the goals of environmental movements. It is important to emphasize that the national state is considered obsolete and past.

Here Falkner refers to a theory by the researcher Daniel Deudney, according to whom environmentalism "produces a powerful cultural shift that leads to a decentring of the nation-state and the growth of cosmopolitan identities" (Falkner 506). Thus, it turns out that *the national state is opposed to green movements and they are fiercely seeking to eliminate it or limit its capacity.* In connection with this, Falkner states that "The very concept of global environmentalism directly challenges the institution of sovereignty. From an ecological perspective, the division of the international system into territorially defined sovereign units is highly problematic" (Falkner 515).

Green movements are successfully trying to incorporate their ideas into legislation. All this is happening without a broad public consensus and even without the knowledge of most people. They only hear about carbon emissions and greenhouse gases every day without having enough information. Yes, the accumulation of rubbish or deforestation is a huge problem and it affects people directly, but global warming or sustainable development are concepts that seem too broad for the average person.

At the same time, international law and international relations are strongly influenced by green ideas. Robert Falkner explains that "International law has gone through a distinct process of greening… Along the way, environmentalism has strengthened the evolution of international law in the direction of more globalist and progressive approaches" (Falkner 519). But is this the right direction of such legislative changes?

As we can see, the basic ideas of green movements are not just about nature and the environment. They have a direct bearing on economics, politics and even culture (as far as education is concerned). They want to apply an integrative approach that can bring together actions in different areas of human activity. According to environmental activists, some common rules and practices must be introduced that are coercive. It does not matter what citizens think- the ambition of environmental movements is above them.

The last sentence, however, should not be taken in an absolute sense. Green movements themselves often ask questions about various issues such as green energy, renewable sources, etc. They question the fact that certain businesses are trying to take advantage of government subsidies and make money that way. *The fact is that big business does not partner directly with green movements*. For example, at Greenpeace we do not see such a partnership. So, we can add another principle - *green movements are suspicious of capitalism and corporations*. They prefer to give more power and authority to ordinary people, to NGOs, to small businesses, to young entrepreneurs.

Here is the place to mention that the activists of the green movements adhere to other ideas, which we can call secondary. This means that these ideas are not essential for environmental movements. Some examples include: vegetarianism and veganism, the use of bicycles and electric cars, the restriction of air travel (and, accordingly, the payment of a special carbon tax), recycling of clothing and other material items, exchange of products and services, carpooling, and more. These ideas are based on the principle of conserving the earth's natural resources. *We need to produce less* because production itself creates waste and it also reduces land resources. Then, we must live according to this principle, without the ambition to be rich or to live well. If we run out of resources, these people say, we will not live normally at all. That is why we must take action now.

Vegetarianism and veganism are traditional practices that originated in India. They are based on the assumption that animals have a soul, so we should not kill them. Killing an animal brings with it bad *karma*, which leads to our rebirth into a lower being in our next life (for example, in Hinduism).

In the last two decades, veganism has become increasingly popular. It denies the consumption of products of animal origin. According to vegans, this reduces greenhouse gas emissions. How exactly does this happen? By raising fewer animals, we waste fewer resources. Also, animals emit gases that can contribute to the greenhouse effect. This is especially true for cattle. Vegans and their colleagues believe that we should give up consuming meat, milk, eggs, cheese, and other similar products. They can be replaced with other foods without adversely affecting our bodies and health.

The idea of riding a bicycle instead of a car is also associated with saving energy and resources. Driving requires a lot of resources, such as fossil fuels. Although a vehicle does not require much, billions of cars around the world need a lot of gasoline. The general picture here is very pessimistic - if the theory of global warming is correct, then it is cars, as well as factories, that will cause such warming through the greenhouse effect. Bicycles, of course, can only be used in urban conditions. It is unthinkable to ride a bicycle hundreds of miles away.

Carpooling is another way to reduce greenhouse gases. These trips reduce the number of vehicles traveling. In addition, it can save money on fuel. These trips have been popular lately in South and North America and Europe - for example BlaBlaCar in Europe, and various web platforms for ridesharing in the United States. Of course, not everyone wants to travel with other people, so the target group is young people who are looking for new contacts and want to save money.

The exchange of unnecessary goods and materials is also exciting. People exchange old things they no longer need - clothes, shoes, furniture, bicycles, and even printers, copiers, tablets, phones. This saves money and wastes fewer resources required to produce these items. This is part of the “circular economy”, which creates little waste and gives little money for various things and services. It is an economy for the poor people, but it also attracts the middle class because it seems morally and socially responsible.

The circular economy has its advantages, too. It really reduces the amount of waste, and it makes it easier for people to have access to things or services they need. This has become facilitated by social networks on the Internet, where users created Web platforms and communicate through them. This movement opposes the tendency to buy new electronic devices every year; they offer the opportunity to buy a cheap and well-functioning device, although already used by another person.

As we can see, all these ideas seem to be interconnected. However, there are logical and practical contradictions between them. We will show this in the following chapters.

1.3 Conclusion

Environmentalism has changed a lot since its beginnings in the 18th century. Of course, it is hard to claim that we can find true environmentalism in Rousseau or Thoreau. Both of them were more like critics of modern civilization with its greediness and egoism.

To be sure, what distinguishes contemporary environmentalism is its strong emphasis on politics. Its proponents try to be connected to policymakers and to influence them all the time. We cannot be certain whether the intentions of the green movements are reasonable and whether they are led simply by moral ideals. At any rate, they are involved in politics and it happens very often that environmentalists become members of the parliament in various countries in the world[5]. American liberals also argue in favor of restrictive policies regarding the use of fossil fuels; thus, the Liberal party has become "green" to some extent.

As we have seen, environmentalists adhere to various principles. Their secondary beliefs may differ, and yet they share core beliefs and principles that are necessarily accepted by them. These principles are taken in a dogmatic way, i.e. as something which does not need any proof. Therefore, we are justified to speak of an ideology, although this is not an entirely political doctrine. We usually perceive ideology as a political thing, but it also includes cultural elements, for example education. Green movements fiercely try to occupy the territory of education in this country. They want to teach their beliefs in all schools, in all colleges.

One of these core beliefs is the theory of global warming. It is so fundamental that it is present everywhere- in textbooks, in media coverages, in the speeches of politicians,

---

[5] This is so especially in Europe- in Germany the Greens are among the leading parties, and in Austria a representative of the Greens was elected a President.

and so forth. All apocalyptic claims by the Greens stem from this theory. Now we turn to the theory of global conception and potential rise in the level of the seawater in the near future. We aim to show that it has not been proved, at least we cannot find enough evidence.

Chapter II: Global warming- human induced or not?

Global warming is a dogma of environmental movements that has a very serious impact on modern economic, social, and even cultural policies. Global warming cannot be disputed; no one has the right to doubt the "arguments" of the green movements about this warming. All modern green politics is motivated by the conception that we must stop global warming. If this alleged global warming continues, then we will live on a planet suffering from floods and natural disasters. American coastal cities will be flooded one day, and we must think about it here and now. This is the "green dogma" to which we will refer in the current chapter.

Our way to deal with the problem is the following: We will look more rationally at the arguments in favor of global warming. In addition, we will focus on other issues such as: how to produce green energy and does it really exist? What would we do if we relied entirely on it alone? We will also add some information on United Nations environmental policies. There we will clearly see that for the United Nations, ecology, poverty, human migration and economic inequality are interrelated problems. This means that refugee waves in our time are justified by natural disasters, which in turn result from global warming. Migration is the result of global warming; therefore, we have to do something about the latter. But what is the truth about all this?

2.1 Arguments for and against the case of global warming

Summary:

We will discuss various points of view and arguments in favor and against the hypothesis of global warming that is induced by humans. We will show that the so-called "anthropogenic theory" has a lot of shortcomings and that it is evident that global warming is not caused (entirely or mostly) by human activity. This is the reason why scientists have been employing the phrase "climate change" recently.

Global warming is the dogma with which environmental movements frighten ordinary people. They paint a terrible picture of a future apocalypse in which many cities will be submerged underwater. It will be a world of melted ice and glaciers, of non-existent winter, of many floods and hurricanes. Some radical environmentalists even claim that there is a risk that the entire human race will disappear. Where is the truth in all this?

It is crucial to note that in the last two decades, *the dogma of global warming has begun to give way to the theory of climate change*. There is already talk that the climate is changing and it is difficult to determine what it will be in the coming decades. This way of talking is replacing what we call global warming. This only shows that critics of global warming were right, and it is essential to approach with doubt this hypothesis that is difficult to prove experimentally and through experience. Today, not many scientists believe that the temperature of the Earth's atmosphere is heading for more severe warming. Instead, it is widely believed that anomalies occur, for example, in one place temperatures rise and in another they fall.

However, we must put stress on the fact that global rise of temperature has been noted for decades. The problem is, what is the reason for this rise?

Another note that every reader should keep in mind is that climate is studied by people who make models and forecasts. Climatology is not an exact science. It has a lot of statistics and math. However, this mathematics is based on the specific data we possess. These data, unfortunately, have been collected for about 150 years, no longer than that. In the past, people were not very interested in air or water temperature; they did not collect enough data, which means that we have to make model predictions about temperatures that existed centuries ago. Therefore, *we do not have precise data about the past; we can only hypothesize about it*.

The problem is that all climate models predict *trends*. For example, we cannot predict exactly what the temperature will be on a particular day in a particular place in one year. Then, we can only deal with probabilities and claim that temperature X is the most probable. Or to claim that in month X temperatures are expected to be higher or lower than average. And that is all we can say!

All this does not mean that climate science is not a science. The problem is that there are factors that cannot always be observed. Accordingly, this leads to changes in the calculations. The Earth's atmosphere is dependent on various solar phenomena. These phenomena can be predicted only after careful observation of the Sun.

We will begin our analysis of the theory of global warming with an interesting phenomenon. Proponents of this theory argue that there is an absolute consensus that no scientist can deny. According to them, it is not the evidence that matters, but the fact that there is a consensus. In a 2016 article, a whole team of scientists is anxious to prove that scientific papers on climate issues have a colossal consensus related to human-induced global warming.

In its response to Richard SJ Tol's critique, the team of scientists argued that "We show that contrary to Tol's claim that the results of C13 differ from earlier studies, the consensus of experts is robust across all studies conducted by co-authors of this correspondence" (Cook et al. 2). This means that according to this team, historical records of C13 (one of the isotopes of carbon) levels in the atmosphere have been interpreted in a similar way by all scientists. The team's thesis is that "The scientific consensus on AGW is robust, with a range of 90% –100% depending on the exact question, timing and sampling methodology. This is supported by multiple independent studies" (Cook et al. 6).

Why is the idea of potential agreement among scientists so important for the green movements? Because, as this team of scientists puts it, "Public perception of scientific consensus has been found to be a gateway belief, affecting other climate beliefs and attitudes including policy support" (Cook et al. 6). In short, the more people believe in this dogma, the easier it will be for others to accept it.

Contrary to the authors' thesis, however, it should be clarified that *consensus is not considered a criterion for truth* - at least not in science. Consensus can only be an additional criterion. It is possible that a consensus supports the wrong theory; most scientists could be wrong (due to external influence, such as political factors). The truth of a theory is based first on facts, and then comes the agreement between scientists. This agreement is important because it shows that these scientists have come to the same conclusion. But *the fact that most scientists support one theory does not in itself mean that this theory is proved forever*. As we can see, most scientists thought that human-induced global warming is real and refused to challenge this dogma. But now most scientists are talking about climate change. This observation shows that there is something wrong with the statement of the aforementioned team of scientists.

We will see later that the voice of scholars opposing this dogma is often not heard. There are such scientists, but for some reason they have not been published, or have been published after a heavy review procedure. *Proponents of human-induced global warming theory do not want to allow anyone to doubt their theory* at all. As the team of scientists puts it, "manufacturing doubt about the scientific consensus on climate change is one of the most effective means of reducing acceptance of climate change and support for mitigation policies" (Cook et al. 6). In short, any doubt must be removed and the scientists who express it censored! Our opinion is that this is not science and has nothing to do with the scientific criteria of truth.

Cook et al. end their article with another controversial statement: "From a broader perspective, it doesn't matter if the consensus number is 90% or 100%. The level of scientific agreement on AGW is overwhelmingly high because the supporting evidence is overwhelmingly strong" (Cook et al. 6). In short, according to this team, global warming is caused by human activity and this is claimed by at least 90% of climate scientists. The question remains, who exactly are these scientists, and if a scientist expresses doubt, how she/he will be taken into account in these statistics?

It must be said that the problem of consensus is very common. In almost every debate on global warming, one of the first arguments to be made is that there is a "general consensus" among all scientists around the world. To this, we find the positions of specific institutions, such as the United Nations, various United Nations agencies dealing with environmental issues, as well as various NGOs operating globally. That is, the green movements prove their theories with the agreement on the topic between the supporters of these movements! Instead of scientists providing the green NGOs with proofs and data, these NGOs provide scientists with pseudo-data and pseudo-facts.

Apocalyptic predictions among the green movements become more frequent when there are fires or high temperatures. An example of this is the fires in the Amazon, Siberia and Australia in 2019, which were used as "evidence" in favor of global warming. Of course, these fires were nothing novel and did not happen for the first time in history. In addition, every summer in Europe and the United States there is talk of the impact of global warming, which makes summer hot. Yes, the last sentence is absurd, because it is normal for summer to be hot and to have high temperatures in summer.

An example of such alarmism is a 2004 article on the severe heat in Europe in the summer of 2003. The authors of this article (Stott, Stone and Allen), published in the prestigious scientific journal *Nature*, claim that this heat proves man-induced global warming and in the future, we will often see similar temperatures not only in summer.

The historical context of this article is the following: A strong heatwave hit Europe in July and August 2003. It is estimated that about 70 000 people died as a result (direct or indirect) of this heatwave. France suffered a lot from the heat, with temperatures above 104 F. Other countries involved were Spain, Portugal, Italy. Rivers in Europe almost became dry. The United Kingdom recorded its record high temperature, (before the heatwave in July 2019). A similar heatwave took place in 2019 in Europe.

The authors claim that according to the observations of all scientists in Europe, this was the hottest summer since 1851. Their position says that the most probable reason for the heatwave is human activity. As they write, "Using a threshold for mean summer temperature that was exceeded in 2003 …we estimate it is very likely … that human influence has at least doubled the risk of a heatwave exceeding this threshold magnitude" (Stott et al. 610). All this is based on the data which we have since 1851. Stott et al. claim that human influence is evident here: "Our analysis shows that European summers are warming owing to anthropogenic climate change. Under un-mitigated emissions scenarios, summers like 2003 are likely to be experienced more frequently in future" (Stott et al. 613).

The alarmism of this team of scientists goes so far as to say that we are about to see even hotter summers, and this is inevitable. As they believe, "with the likelihood of such events projected to increase 100-fold over the next four decades, it is difficult to avoid the conclusion that potentially dangerous anthropogenic interference in the climate system is already underway" (Stott et al. 613). But all this is just probabilities! In addition, the predictions made by such scientists are inaccurate. The following summers after 2003 were far cooler and wetter. Even the summer of 2021 was relatively cool in the United States and Europe. Only 2006 and 2019 were exceptions, during which record values were recorded in Europe.

It is also important to say that similar record temperatures are not observed everywhere at the same time. They are found only in small regions. In 2003, for example, the heat engulfed countries with warmer climates. In the Scandinavian countries, for example, no records were set. If there really was global warming and it was visible everywhere and always, then the whole of Europe would be engulfed in heat. However, such examples are used as false evidence by radical green activists who never turn to real data. When a summer is cooler than usual, they talk about climate change. When it is hotter than normal, for them it is perfect proof of global warming.

In another article for the scientific journal *Science*, the researcher David King refers to the hot summer of 2003 and states that "when average temperatures are rising, extreme temperatures become more frequent and more serious… Climate change is the most severe problem that we are facing today — more serious even than the threat of terrorism" (King 176). This comparison to terrorism is very curious because it shows how far radical environmentalists or alarmists can go. They want to ignore any other threats to our society, so only global warming remains real. The most important thing is to deal with it, and everything else must be set aside!

David King goes on by saying that over the last 200 years "human activity has increased the atmospheric concentration of greenhouse gases by some 50% relative to preindustrial levels. At about 372 ppm, today's atmospheric carbon dioxide level is higher than at any time in at least the past 420,000 years" (King 176). But is this data precise? We should not think so.

Of course, we do not have accurate data for the last 400 millennia, but scientists have certain models. They believe that these models reflect the facts and that the Earth is really warming all these years. But *the presence of a certain amount of carbon in the atmosphere does not automatically mean that it is due to human activity*. This presence cannot be disputed because it can be measured in real terms; the problem is that we obtained our data on it recently, and we cannot tell what the data of all these 400,000 years is. How can we be sure that (1) this is indeed the highest level of carbon in the atmosphere for this period, and that (2) this is due to human activity? These are questions that still raise doubts and lead to disagreement among scientists. As we have already seen, the conception of absolute consensus is not correct- something that we will prove a little further in this chapter.

The idea of the interdependence between global warming, poverty and migration is easily seen in the works of various scientists, although poverty is not their subject of study. In the following quote, the reader can notice the political line that is present. As King says, if we continue to use fossil fuels, which in turn will lead to rising temperatures around the world, "the numbers of additional people exposed to frequent flooding in river delta areas such as the Nile… and from coastline cities and villages of India, Japan, and the Philippines, would be counted in hundreds of millions" (King 176). These floods will affect countries in Asia and Africa the most, but according to the author, the United States and Europe will not get along easily. They will also suffer greatly, as a result of a global natural disaster. It can be avoided if we take action now and as soon as possible.

The leftist beliefs of some scientists working on climate change are easily noticeable. In another article, the scientists Diffenbaugh and Burke expressed the view that climate change is leading to greater poverty and social inequality. They believe that "rich countries" are to blame for this poverty because they produce a lot of greenhouse gases. Diffenbaugh and Burke state that "Given that wealthy countries have been responsible for the vast majority of historical greenhouse gas emissions, any clear evidence of inequality in the impacts of the associated climate change raises critical questions of international justice" (Diffenbaugh, Burke (9808).

Justice means that rich countries must help the poorer with climate change, based on the hypothesis that rich countries are to blame for global warming, as opposed to poor people who are simply its "victims." The question remains whether countries like China or Brazil are held to be "poor." They are among the biggest polluters, so they should also take responsibility for this pollution and the current environmental crisis.

According to the authors in question, there is an inverse relationship between economic growth and climate change. They argue that wealthy countries will become even wealthier thanks to the appropriate climatic conditions, while poor countries will suffer from various natural disasters and will not be able to rely on themselves economically. They state that "The estimated parabolic relationship between temperature and economic growth means that long-term warming will generally increase growth in cool countries and decrease growth in warm countries" (Diffenbaugh, Burke 9809).

It is not very clear whether such a ratio really exists, or whether it is simply a hypothesis of left-leaning researchers on environmental issues. These authors add the controversial hypothesis that "the poorest half of the population-weighted country-level economic distribution has become relatively more poor over the 1961–2010 period" (Diffenbaugh, Burke 9810).

It is obvious that environmental catastrophes lead to migration, impoverishment of the population, as well as to fear of similar disasters in the future. But the hypothesis of global warming as a result of human activity has not yet been proved by scientific methods. This means that we cannot blame rich countries for creating environmental disasters for poorer countries. This is simply not true. It can even be said the opposite - rich countries establish special funds to support poorer countries around the world. Richer countries today produce and disseminate new technologies that are environmentally friendly. These technologies are provided to poor countries for little money or even for free. It is not at all true that rich countries hinder poor nations. In fact, the only hope of the poor is that the richer countries will lend a hand. And this is exactly what is happening nowadays!

One possible explanation for the impoverishment of poor countries in recent decades can be seen in the following quote: "Many countries in our sample have experienced rapid urbanization and economic development for reasons unrelated to climate, and such trends could plausibly alter how economies respond to subsequent climate change" (Diffenbaugh, Burke 9811). That is why it is difficult to prove whether this impoverishment is entirely due to climate change (as it undoubtedly exists) or something else. The rapid population growth of certain countries leads to unequal distribution of resources and mass poverty. If we add to this the poor level of education, as well as corruption in very poor countries, this already explains where this impoverishment comes from.

And while acknowledging that climate change does not have such a clear impact on impoverishment, these authors argue that the blame is ultimately on the richer countries and they should be held accountable for all these negative processes. As they say, "not only have poor countries not shared in the full benefits of energy consumption, but many have already been made poorer (in relative terms) by the energy consumption of wealthy countries" (Diffenbaugh, Burke 9812). But this is not true, because wealthy countries provide technology and money to Third World countries.

The dogmatic adherence to the thesis that global warming is due entirely to human activity can also be seen in the article "Understanding and Attributing Climate Change" (2007) by G.C. Hegerl and his team of researchers from the UK. The main thesis of the article is that "It is extremely unlikely (<5%) that the global pattern of warming during the past half century can be explained without external forcing, and very unlikely that it is due to known natural external causes alone." According to this team, human activity is the only possible explanation: "The warming occurred in both the ocean and the atmosphere and took place at a time when natural external forcing factors would likely have produced cooling" (Hegerl et al. 665).

Hegerl et al. claim that computer simulations show exactly the relationship between human activity and the real indications of global warming. They write that "There is much greater similarity between the general evolution of warming in observations and that simulated by models when anthropogenic and natural forcings are included than when only natural forcing is included" (Hegerl et al. 685). In short, we have computer models and simulations that show some resemblance to reality; but this has been the reality only in recent years.

The dogmatic attitude of the advocates of the green ideology is seen in the next paragraph, where the authors talk about the Earth's past and that such warming has already taken place. At the same time, according to them, the current warming is unique: "The Earth system has experienced large-scale climate changes in the past that hold important lessons for the understanding of present and future climate change. These changes resulted from natural external forcings that ... triggered strong feedbacks" (Hegerl et al. 679). Therefore, such warmings happened in the past, but the warming in the 20th and 21st centuries is something extraordinary. Should we all agree with this?

However, there is no lack of specific research on certain regions of the planet. One of the most interesting questions is whether the glaciers of Antarctica are melting.

The data are contradictory - when a glacier melts, a real hysteria begins in the midst of green movements. At the same time, if the temperatures turn out to be even lower than expected, there is no reaction from them. The same, as we have noted, is happening with fires and floods in different parts of the world.

In an article by David Vaughan et al. (2003), we find some interesting facts about this part of our planet. According to them, the warming of this continent is obvious. They begin their publication with the dogmatic statement, "The Intergovernmental Panel on Climate Change has determined that global warming, the average warming of the planet's surface, was 0.6 ± 0.2 ◦C during the 20th century" (Vaughan et al. 243). They argue that, for this reason, we must take urgent measures to avoid a global cataclysm.

This team of scientists claims that "Station records show that the Antarctic Peninsula has warmed at 3.7 ± 1.6 ◦C (century) −1, several times the rate of global warming and quite different to most of the other station records from the Antarctic continent." At the same time, according to them, the warming of this peninsula is not something extraordinary. If we look at the historical records of temperatures on this continent, "we find no evidence for a 'polar amplification 'of climate change elsewhere in Antarctica. Rather, we see a regionally variable pattern, with an underlying warming not significantly different to the global mean" (Vaughan et al. 267). This is a recognition of the difficulty of proving the hypothesis of melting glaciers in the near future and the corresponding rise in the level of the world's oceans.

The authors make another important statement: "The undoubted advances of recent years in reproducing global warming are impressive, but these models are not yet ready to provide us with a reliable basis for planning national adaptation and mitigation, and should be improved with utmost haste" (Vaughan et al. 268).

As we have already shown, in recent years the theory of global warming caused entirely by human intervention has not been considered scientifically sound. There is more talk of climate change. In his 2011 article, one of the few critics of this theory to be allowed to publish in a peer-reviewed journal, Norman Paterson, shared his arguments against the idea that man is causing global warming. The researcher Paterson, in his article "Global Warming: A Critique of the Anthropogenic Model and its Consequences", criticizes the dogmatism of environmental movements and their attempts to influence research in this field.

Norman Paterson begins his publication as follows: "We are led today by our media, governments, schools and some scientific authorities to believe that, through his CO2 emissions, man is entirely… responsible for the modest, modulated rise in global temperature of about 0.7 ° C." He goes on to with the assertion that "We are told, and many sincere people believe, that if we continue on this path, the planet will experience escalating temperature and dangerous sea level rise before the end of this century" (Paterson 41-42).

Here Paterson begins to present his clearly formulated arguments. He begins with the proven statement that "Geological records show unequivocally that past temperature increases have always preceded, not followed, increases in CO2; i.e. the warming could potentially cause the CO2 increase, but not the reverse" (Paterson 42). This statement is interesting because it offers another hypothesis for global warming - that it actually leads to an increase in greenhouse gases. In short, the problem of scientists today is how they interpret the causal relationship between one phenomenon and another. Which is first and which is second? Are carbon emissions increasing first? For, if this is not the case, then man is not (mainly) to blame for global warming; therefore, this warming will not last long and soon the Earth will become cooler.

Paterson points out that "It is likely that the cyclical warming and cooling of the earth results from a number of different causes, none of which, taken alone, is dominant enough to be entirely responsible." According to him, this shows that human activity cannot be considered the only or even the dominant factor in this aspect. Some factors rarely discussed among green activists are "solar changes (including both irradiance and magnetic field effects), atmosphere – ocean interaction (including both multidecadal climatic oscillations and unforced internal variability), and greenhouse gases" (Paterson 42).

It is curious (and inexplicable) that these factors are often overlooked, and in textbooks and in the media they are not even mentioned! The author even notes that the IPCC (Intergovernmental Panel on Climate Change) focuses mainly on the role of human activity, the greenhouse gas emissions in relation to this activity. He writes that "All of these factors have been discussed by the IPCC, but the first two have been dismissed as negligible in comparison with the greenhouse-gas effect and man's contribution to it through anthropogenic CO2" (Paterson 42).

This Geneva-based institute is known for its activities in support of the human factor theory and its fervent support for reducing greenhouse gas emissions through strict restrictions. Contrary to its reports, Paterson claims the following: "Both solar irradiation and ocean – atmosphere oscillations have therefore been demonstrated to have effects on global temperature of at least the same order of magnitude as the CO2 greenhouse gas hypothesis" (Paterson 44). But preference is given only to scientists that emphasize the human factor; nothing else is important to the representatives of this institute. The question remains, is this institute scientific at all, or is it rather political?

In this case, the Canadian scholar remarks that "Politics also plays an important part in the controversy, and a high value is placed on political correctness... The situation is worsened because, very often, a scientific reputation or a career is at stake" (Paterson 45). This is the reason for the "consensus" in question, which we have already mentioned - many scientists are censored because their hypotheses and observations do not correspond to the theory of the human factor. Even if there is a slight discrepancy between their theory and what is supported by the IPCC, they are censored, i.e. publications in peer-reviewed journals are not allowed. This really seems to be a political problem, because there is no other explanation. A scientist must conduct their research according to valid and current knowledge, and not according to the dominant dogmatic attitude (not even theory). And the theory of global warming caused mainly by man is not well proved, i.e. it cannot be called scientific.

Again, *the huge problem here is the difficulty of observing the process of warming over a longer period*. Only 150 years ago, we started doing such research, which leads to many knowledge deficits. And this is where Norman Paterson asserts that "claims by IPCC and others that 1998 was the warmest year on record ignore the data from 1500 and earlier, and also fail to point out that 1998 was the year of strongest ocean / atmospheric effect, known as El Niño" (Paterson 45). In short, older data are deliberately ignored simply because they lead to confusion and doubt about the validity of the dogma of the anthropogenic factor.

At the end of his article, the author points out that we need to reconsider our attitude towards climate change and introduce green energy into our lives more slowly. You have to think in the long run. As he puts it, “anti-CO2 measures manifest themselves, in the short term, in costly energy alternatives and CO2 remission or sequestration programs. Energy conservation and market efficiencies will ... dictate the use of alternative energy sources such as geothermal” (Paterson 46). It is more important to make energy consumption more economical and to limit energy waste.

There is another publication that criticizes the hysteria surrounding the anthropogenic factor. Michael Schellenberger (2019) exposes his moderate critique of the hysteria provoked by more radical green activists. According to him, some activists present ideas that have nothing to do with science. *They represent an apocalyptic vision that has no scientific basis*. Many journalists and green activists are to blame for this. As he writes, “Bill McKibben suggested climate-driven fires in Australia had made koalas’ functionally extinct. *Extinction Rebellion* said ‘Billions will die’ and ‘Life on Earth is dying.’ *Vice* claimed the ‘collapse of civilization may have already fled’” (Shellenberger par. 1). To these we can add the climate strike of Greta Thunberg, a young activist who at the end of 2019 even gave a speech at the annual United Nations conference in New York. In short, humanity is disappearing just because it uses fossil fuels!

Schellenberger writes that “no credible scientific body has ever said climate change threatens the collapse of civilization much less the extinction of the human species” (Shellenberger par. 10). Koalas have not disappeared yet and, the fires at the end of 2019 in Australia did not threaten their existence. Besides all this, natural disasters are not something novel for us. As this journalist observes, "it's also true that economic development has made us less vulnerable, which is why there was a 99.7% decline in the death toll from natural disasters since its peak in 1931" (Schellenberger par. 10).

These statements remind us that in fact the world is moving toward the better. It is not at all true that it is moving toward some kind of world catastrophe. The world's population is increasing and life expectancy is increasing as well. In short, we live better than our ancestors a hundred years ago. How then can we talk about a global catastrophe and even the destruction of the human race? This is a real absurdity and is based on emotions (mostly fear) and not on scientific facts.

As Schellenberger reports, "In 1931, 3.7 million people died from natural disasters. In 2018, just 11,000 did. And that decline occurred over a period when the global population was quadrupled" (Shellenberger par. 18 and 19). All this only shows that we have no serious cause for concern. In fact, radical anthropogenic hypotheses argue that this apocalypse will happen soon. But do we see how it is happening right now? Do we see its signs? Are there endangered species dying in any region of planet Earth? The answer is only no.

There are many other claims by radical green activists that can easily be refuted. They talk about mass hunger and poverty. As Shellenberger says, "What about claims of crop failure, famine, and mass death? That's science fiction, not science. Humans today produce enough food for 10 billion people, or 25% more than we need, and scientific bodies predict increases in that share, not declines" (Shellenberger par. 22). This means that we will have better and better technologies that will help us use our resources more efficiently. By reducing energy costs and by allocating resources more practically, we (all of humanity) will be able to better control our lives. Instead of hunger and poverty, we can hope for a good life in which our needs will be met.

Yes, climate change can lead to certain problems. This includes natural disasters and economic damage. As Shellenberger mentions, "Climate change may threaten one million species globally and half of all mammals, reptiles, and amphibians in diverse places like the Albertine Rift in central Africa, home to the endangered mountain gorilla" (Shellenberger par. 28). We must take care of all animal species, because their existence is crucial for harmony in nature. The extinction of even unsightly species can have serious consequences. But according to this author, climate change will not lead to such extinction; or, if certain species become extinct, it will be the result of something else (for example, because they are directly endangered by humans).

Radical green activists sometimes express absurd views that contradict their leftist beliefs. For example, they believe that fossil fuels should be banned, which will lead to many problems for poorer nations. As Shellenberger notes, "Part of what bothers me about the apocalyptic rhetoric by climate activists is that it is often accompanied by demands that poor nations be denied the cheap sources of energy they need to develop. I have found that many scientists share my concerns" (Shellenberger para. 45). We need to think rationally when it comes to environmental issues. We cannot solve all of them at once. We can do it gradually and with a clear vision. We should not be led by fear - this is the conclusion of this journalist.

According to Shellenberger, we need to find moderate solutions to the environmental problems that concern us today. Radical decisions cannot be made because they are not reasonable. We can neither completely ban fossil fuels nor ignore environmental issues. As we will see later in this book, man is a part of nature and cannot afford to destroy it. However, this destruction must be seen in a different context, such as deforestation, soil, water and air pollution. Alleged global warming will not lead to the extinction of the species, because it will stop at some point, and then cooling will occur. Such is the balance in nature. Shellenberger states as follows: "Happily, there is a plenty of middle ground between climate apocalypse and climate denial" (Shellenberger par. 50).

In conclusion, the journalist exposes an interesting fact that is often ignored. The IPCC estimates that the global economy will not decline, but will actually improve: "By 2100, IPCC projects the global economy will be 300 to 500% larger than it is today... Warming of 2.5 ° C and 4 ° C would reduce gross domestic product (GDP) by 2% and 5% over that same period" (Shellenberger par. 26). What about the hypothesis that climate change will make all of us poorer?

Shellenberger's view should not be seen as a denial of climate change or the fact that there is global warming. He simply questions the anthropogenic factor in warming and says we need to think more sensibly. Man is a rational being and has achieved many things thanks to his reason. Emotions are an essential part of our lives, but they must be controlled and balanced with reason, with the rational. History of environmental movements is usually full of apocalyptic predictions and images, as J.R. McNeill remarks. He points out that "A criticism sometimes leveled at environmental history is that its narratives are relentlessly depressing accounts of environmental destruction: just one damn decline after another" (McNeill 35). We need to have a more optimistic look at nature and the environment, and to believe in our ability to overcome the current crisis.

This moderate approach should be applied to the problem of the so-called green energy, or energy that comes from renewable sources. It is also linked to the problem of sustainability. What is the connection between these two things and what is the perspective of green energy?

2.2 Renewable energy: A bright future or a menace for mankind?

Summary:

Here we will demonstrate that the so-called green energy is not enough to maintain our power demands. The case with Texas in 2021 shows that this type of energy is not reliable. There are also other points that we will emphasize in the current subchapter.

Green activists say we need to limit the use of fossil fuels and replace them with energy from renewable sources - sun, wind, water, biomass, and more. They claim that in this way we will get rid of our dependence on fossil fuels and we will be able to have endless resources - because, according to them, solar, wind and hydro energy are inexhaustible. They call "green" the energy produced from renewable energy technologies. However, this perspective requires serious discussion. In this regard, we must ask the following questions:

1. Can we rely entirely on green energy?

2. Is it possible that green energy is also harmful to nature?

3. Should we limit energy use at all? The Greens believe that we should impose such restrictions and rely only on green energy.

Most green activists and NGOs confidently (and dogmatically) claim that green energy is our clear and happy future. According to them, it will improve our lives and reduce poverty, as well as lead to a fair distribution of resources. The gap between rich and poor people will narrow due to the fact that the poor will need fewer resources.

Let's imagine a situation where all poor households have technologies that allow them to easily heat the air and water in their homes, as well as have electricity. If these technologies are cheap or even free, these people will be able to easily reduce their budget and spend money only on food. Energy has a major share in the budget of Third World nations, except for those who are constantly warm. But anyway, these people also need electricity, and it has to come from somewhere. Green activists say this energy will be cheap and easily accessible. It is only necessary for global businesses to invest in the technologies that will produce it.

But here comes the problem of whether such an investment is worth it. If green energy is very expensive, then what is the point to replace fossil fuels and nuclear energy? And we see that the technologies for its production are expensive, which automatically leads to a higher cost of energy itself.

At the moment, there is fierce political pressure to switch entirely to green energy, the consequences of which will not be very good. Situations such as the crisis in Texas in February 2021 will be taking place very often. But what actually happened in Texas?

The presentation of this crisis in the major media is indicative of the pressure in favor of green energy. Although it is obvious that this crisis was caused by the excessive share of green energy in the energy system of Texas, the mass media in the United States claim that the reason is quite different. Let's see what it is, according to them.

Here we will refer to a publication by AP prepared by Nomaan Merchant. The power crisis that occurred in the state of Texas in February 2021 is described as follows: "As temperatures plunged and snow and ice whipped the state, much of Texas' power grid collapsed, followed by its water systems. Tens of millions huddled in frigid homes that slowly grew colder or fled for safety" (Merchant par. 3). The author describes the extraordinary cold wave from which Texas suffered: "And a prideful state, long suspicious of regulation and outside help, was left to seek aid from other states and humanitarian groups as many of its 29 million people grasped for survival" (Merchant par. 3).

Although we are talking about an extreme phenomenon, Merchant immediately turns to the political context of the crisis and indirectly blames the Republican Party for it: "The state's Republican leadership was blamed for ignoring warnings that winter could wreak the havoc that it did, and for not providing local officials with enough information to protect residents now". He goes on to say that "A lack of regulations to protect critical infrastructure and failure by officials to take recommended steps to winterize equipment left the nation's largest energy-producing state unprepared for last week's weather emergency" (Merchant par. 6).

But is all this due to the Republican Party? Here we can recall the serious allegations against President George Bush over Hurricane Katrina in 2005. One gets the feeling that *all these accusations have a political purpose*.

Governor Abbott was harshly criticized by liberal media and activists for his sincere declaration regarding the energy crisis. As Merchant points out, "Abbott blamed this week's fiasco on green energy… Abbott did note failures across the energy industry. But others among the Republican leadership continued to tweet condemnations of green energy or support for natural gas" (Merchant par. 44). Green energy has indeed been introduced in the state of Texas recently with the idea of making it even more independent of the federal energy system. This type of energy had to provide the necessary power even in such crises. That is why Governor Abbott shows his critical attitude towards this type of energy - it is energy that cannot be relied on entirely. Of course, we are talking about an exceptional event and one of the coldest winters in history.

And yet, the Republican Party is proved to be the main culprit for the crisis! The problem does not lie in the very essence of green energy, which in general cannot provide the necessary capacity in such a crisis that emerged suddenly. As the author writes, "Despite efforts by some Republicans to blame clean energy, the failures occurred in every part of the sector. While wind turbines and solar panels froze, a major nuclear plant lost half of its generation, and there were massive failures in coal, oil, and natural gas" (Merchant par. 38). But all this is not due to fossil fuels or nuclear energy, but to the fact that these fuels are not used enough because of the “green” political pressure. If they had not been curtailed for many years, such a crisis simply would not have existed, or at least not on this scale.

The explanation of the author of this publication is that Texas is too isolated, which is why it cannot connect to the federal energy network. As he notes, “There is a long and colorful history to how this came to be, but the simplest explanation is that Texas utilities wanted to be free of federal regulation. They accomplished that ... by avoiding sending power across state lines” (Merchant par. 33). In short, everything else is to blame but green energy!

It is clear that this publication is biased and it aims to defend the concept of green energy. But the author must answer two critical questions:

1. Why is such a crisis happening for the first time, and right now, when the capacity of nuclear energy is reduced?

2. Where is the place of global warming? Why in hot months we are constantly reminded of this warming, and when there are cold winters, we hear nothing about it?

The sound conclusion from all this is that (at least for now) *green energy cannot provide the capacity we need*. And the problem is not the energy isolation of Texas, but that we are reducing our own energy resources just to meet the demands of green activists and green businesses. Renewable energy should be introduced gradually, but it should not have a large share in our energy system. It simply does not have the technological capacity to deal with such cold winters or other exceptional climatic events.

Moreover, scientists defending the concept of green energy wrote very different things 20 years ago. In their 2002 publication, Pimentel et al. write that "The first priority of the US energy program should be for individuals, communities, and industries to conserve fossil fuel resources by using renewable resources and by reducing consumption" (Pimentel et al. 1117). According to them, the United States is already far behind in this regard: "Other developed countries have implemented that high productivity and a high standard of living can be achieved with the use of half of the energy expenditure of the United States" (Pimentel et al. 1117).

The position of this team of scientists is that U.S. resources are depleting and a new type of energy must be considered. According to them, "The United States, having consumed from 82% to 88% of its proved oil reserves (API 1999), now imports more than 60% of its oil at an annual cost of approximately $ 75 billion" (Pimentel et al. 1111). That is a fact - the United States does import too much fossil fuel. But all this does not mean that we should immediately switch to green energy. This team of scientists in its article highlights some weak points of green energy. Their position is objective because it shows that "green technologies" can also be directed against nature and green resources.

One such example of a contradiction is hydroelectric power. According to the observation of Pimentel et al., "Plants cause major environmental problems. The impounded water frequently covers valuable, agriculturally productive, alluvial bottomland. Furthermore, dams alter the existing plants, animals, and microbes in the ecosystem" (Pimentel et al. 1112). In heavy rainfall, dams can lead to terrible floods, so they must be carefully monitored. In addition, there are countries in the world where water is a scarce resource and cannot afford to use this type of energy. Is it moral to turn water into electricity instead of using it for drinking?

Another problem is wind energy. Wind turbines interfere with the normal life of birds and other animals inhabiting the area. As Pimentel et al. point out, “Locating the wind turbines in or near the flyways of migrating birds and wildlife refuges may result in birds colliding with the supporting towers and rotating blades” (Pimentel et al. 1113). To all this we must add two facts: (1) The construction of turbines requires a lot of (non-green) energy, and (2) Their transport is usually expensive, which means that resources are wasted. Besides, turbines reduce their capacity over time and need to be repaired frequently. In general, wind turbines are not really a green type of energy.

Photovoltaic technology is another way to produce electricity. However, it has two weak points. First, photovoltaics occupy vast areas of land. This land can be used for agriculture instead of electricity. And secondly, some of the materials needed for their production are toxic. As Pimentel et al. Write, “The major environmental problem associated with photovoltaic systems is the use of toxic chemicals, such as cadmium sulfide and gallium arsenide, in their manufacture” (Pimentel et al. 1115). They explain that “Because these chemicals are highly toxic and persist in the environment for centuries, disposal and recycling of materials in inoperative cells could become a major problem.” Photovoltaics can be very important for the energy independence of individual households because they allow these households to generate electricity themselves. But they, like most other types of green energy, have their weaknesses.

Last but not least, Pimenetel et al. note that a huge problem related to green energy is infrastructure. As they write, “An additional complication in the transition to renewable energies is the relationship between the location of ideal production sites and large population centers." It turns out that this energy is more difficult to reach large cities: "Ideal locations for renewable energy technologies are often remote, such as deserts of the American Southwest or wind farms located kilometers offshore" (Pimentel et al. 1117). Wind turbines, photovoltaics, and other green energy production sites cannot be located inside large cities. Therefore, this is a problem that needs to be solved.

Therefore, we come to the conclusion that green energy is necessary for some reasons. We do not know exactly what the motives of the green activists are, but we can safely talk about a green lobby. At the same time, new treaties and agreements are being adopted in the international arena, aimed at reducing carbon emissions and protecting the planet from presumed global warming. We will now talk a little about green pressure at the international level.

2.3 The international Green lobby: United Nations and other international institutions

Summary:

Here we will analyze the activities of the United Nations related to reducing greenhouse emissions. We will answer the question, who has the right to control these emissions and what to do with poor countries.

In the First chapter, we pointed out that the new green wave is not only ecologically but also politically oriented. Unlike the first environmental activists, green activists today are politicians and fighters. They are fighting both nationally and internationally. They often create cross-border associations that operate simultaneously in their countries. An example of this is Greenpeace, which insists that borders must be erased and we must all unite in the name of the common goal of saving planet Earth and life on it.

International law is something very complicated. There is no way to impose "environmental sanctions" on particular countries. This means that each country can decide for itself how to treat these problems. No one has the right to put pressure on a given country unless the latter itself has already signed a contract. Such are, for example, the Kyoto Protocols (1997) and the Paris Agreement (2015), signed by almost all countries in the world. However, these international treaties have no criminal function - there is no court that imposes fines on the signatory states. In addition, any country can withdraw from them, as Canada did in 2012.

The Kyoto protocols are based on the conception of reducing greenhouse gases emissions to a certain extent and level. The countries that ratified the Protocols have definite binding targets, which means that they should act quickly and control what they do. The Protocols (promoted by the United Nations) oblige developed countries (including the whole European Union) that ratified this agreement to reduce their emissions from 5 to 8 %, depending on the particular country.

It is very curious that China was held to be a "developing country" in the 1990s, so it does not have any binding targets. The United States are not part of the Protocols since they have not been ratified yet because of the fact that huge industries like India and China are not obliged in any way to reduce their emissions. This is not fair, and the United States cannot allow this to happen.

In an interesting article concerning the failure of the Kyoto Protocols, the researcher Amanda Rosen notes several features that made the Protocols flawed in themselves. According to her, they were prepared prematurely by the United Nations, without having a good strategy. Not the countries that did not meet their targets are to blame. As she points out, “The real culprit, however, is not the states that failed to join but the very design of the treaty itself, which stacked the deck against success in mitigating climate change now and in the future” (Rosen 31). Pretending to have achieved some success, the parties of the agreement are blind to the fact that these effects are not measured properly. The Protocols are formulated only in a short-term perspective, which itself makes them futile. As Rosen claims, “By focusing on the short term for the last 15 years, we have lost out on 15 years of large scale changes in land, transportation, and energy use as well as the innovation and experimentation that should have been going on during that time” (Rosen 44).

To be sure, most of the parties have not achieved their targets. As Rosen observes, “Canadian carbon dioxide emissions increased by 25 percent from 1990 to 2012 and Japan’s emissions increased by 14 percent over the same period.”[6] On the other hand, the EU countries are much more efficient: “The success rate improves when we turn our attention to Europe, however, which achieved a 15 percent reduction in emissions from 1990 levels in the EU-15, well beyond the 8 percent target set for that group” (Rosen 36). But the fact that a certain country is not a party of the Protocols does not mean that it does not do anything against climate change. The United States perform well in this respect by investing in new technologies, reducing greenhouse gases emissions,

[6] This is the reason for the withdrawal of Canada from the Protocols. With increasing GHG emissions, Canada could be subjected to penalties under the agreement.

promoting hybrids and electric vehicles. Amanda Rosen remarks that "Within the United States there are regional cap-and-trade programs… carbon taxes, substantial emission reduction targets, incentives and regulations on renewable energy consumption, and increasing automobile emission standards" (Rosen 37).

All this means that the Kyoto protocols themselves cannot change anything; countries should be actively involved to help mankind adapt to climate changes. Why should the U.S. ratify the Protocols if America has taken the necessary measures to achieve targets similar to those defined in the Protocols? As Amanda Rosen puts it, "Several of these programs preceded Kyoto; the others were created despite U.S. nonparticipation in the regime" (Rosen 37).

The short-term perspective of the Protocols is the main problem. They aimed to reach several goals by 2008, and after that another Annex was added, with goals to achieve by 2020. But such a transformation of the energy system cannot take place at once; it needs decades! As we have seen, the "green revolution" can only take place gradually. We cannot eliminate all fossil fuels; we cannot deprive ourselves of nuclear energy. We will need this energy later, during the cold winters that will happen (without any doubt) in the future. As Rosen remarks, "Kyoto incentivized measures that produce identifiable emission reductions in the short term rather than encouraging the pursuit of more fundamental policy changes and investments that could have produced greater reductions in the long run" (Rosen 39).

For example, some countries went from using oil to using natural gas, which also is related to greenhouse gases. They reduced their emissions, but in long term they will have some impact on these emissions. Natural gas could be used for conducting a transition from an economy based on fossil fuels to an entirely "green" economy, but it has its weak points.

The conclusion is evident: we need to prepare an excellent, far-reaching strategy to be realized within the following decades. We cannot rely on chaotic data or emotions. We have to get rid of the idea that the world will end in a few years due to global warming. We have plenty of time to take action and our actions need to be well justified and practical. *We cannot suddenly ban all fossil fuels or nuclear energy.* We cannot simply replace our cars with electrical cars. But we are able to promote hybrid cars, new technologies; systems for saving power and resources. On the other hand, all members of the United Nations must take measures to stop the contamination of air, water and soil by China, India, Brazil and other "developing countries." It is time to say enough to them, and to tell them that they are not free from environmental obligations.

As Amanda Rosen concludes, "What the Kyoto experience teaches us is that the wrong international agreement can undermine the entire effort to solve a global problem-even it comes at the right time" (Rosen 46). This means, agreements are not enough; there should be a conceptual framework behind them. We need to predict the consequences of our actions and measure their efficiency. Today, we rarely hear about Kyoto; the parties of this agreement have simply forgotten about it.

The Paris Agreement is similar to the Kyoto Protocols, but it adds new dimensions and new data. Withdrawing from this agreement is a simple process and was made by President Trump. The problem is that any participation in this Agreement could do some damage to the economy of the United States; and this is a problem that we cannot analyze in-depth here. All we should say is that all economies should be treated equally, and there should not be advantages for the "developing" ones.

Regarding all these international agreements, we can say that they are based on goodwill. The countries that ratify them want to join the struggle for the salvation of the planet. The agreements themselves are not a problem. The problem is in the propaganda of certain actions that actually damage the economy. These actions have been promoted without any criticism and doubt in them.

An example of such propaganda is a program implemented by the United Nations. It was adopted in 2000 and called Millennium Development Goals. It consists of achieving certain goals that will make the world a better place for everyone. It has goals such as: poverty reduction, child mortality reduction, the fight against AIDS and malaria, as well as public education. One of the goals is about achieving sustainability, which includes combating global warming. The United Nations gives money to all nations to achieve these goals gradually. There are particular tasks and targets to be reached. Every country has to reach their targets in a timely manner.

However, this is difficult to achieve and that is why this program was recently renewed under the name 2030 Agenda for Sustainable Development. It is more comprehensive than its previous version and has more "green" goals. The purpose of this whole Agenda is to act internationally in many different areas, because environmental issues are not solved on their own. In order for people to use green technology, they must be able to afford it. Poverty and disease also make a decisive contribution here because they have a direct impact on the state of the environment.

In the Introduction to this plan, we see the following thesis: "This Agenda is a plan of action for people, planet and prosperity ... We recognize that eradicating poverty in all its forms and dimensions, including extreme poverty, is the greatest global challenge and an indispensable requirement for sustainable development" (UN 3). In short, poverty and inequality are the biggest problems in the world, from which everyone else stems. The idea is that poverty leads to conflicts, and resource shortages can be dangerous for all regions of the world.

These new 17 Goals "seek to build on the Millennium Development Goals and complete what they did not achieve. They seek to realize the human rights of all and to achieve gender equality and the empowerment of all women and girls" (UN 3). Here we also see the conception of gender inequality (which is real in some parts of the planet) and the need to eliminate it as much as possible.

Without a doubt, the United Nations is an organization that stands close to some leftist ideas but it is not leftist in itself. The conception of reducing world poverty has never been left-wing. The Catholic Church, for example, also fights poverty. But the idea of universal equality in every aspect, in every possible sphere, is left-wing. This should make us aware that it is not so easy to say that a certain organization is "left-wing" or "right-wing."

In addition, the United Nations must diplomatically maneuver between different ideologies adhered to by different governments around the world. This Agenda attempts to bring us closer to certain goals, but achieving them is so far utopian and difficult. For example, Pakistan cannot be forced to introduce a special law on complete equality between men and women. This can only be done with external pressure, which is quite controversial.

Along with poverty and inequality, as well as social injustice, this Agenda aims to "ensure the lasting protection of the planet and its natural resources" (UN 4). Further, we read that "We resolve also to create conditions for sustainable, inclusive and sustained economic growth, shared prosperity and decent work for all, taking into account different levels of national development and capacities" (UN 4). Economic development must be looked at differently, in the context of poverty, inequality and environmental problems.

Reducing greenhouse gas emissions is proving to be one of the main goals of this Agenda. We read that "The global nature of climate change calls for the widest possible international cooperation aimed at accelerating the reduction of global greenhouse gas emissions and addressing adaptation to the adverse impacts of climate change" (UN 10). Interestingly, we are already talking about climate change here, not global warming based on human activity. Elsewhere, it is mentioned that greenhouse gas reduction rates are not enough and that the signatories to this Agenda need to better stick to their promises (UN 10). The idea is to stop global warming to a maximum of 2 degrees Celsius above pre-industrial levels of carbon in the atmosphere.

Besides all this, in this text we can find the following Goals related to the environment:

-Goal 6: Ensure availability and sustainable management of water and sanitation for all.

-Goal 7: Ensure access to affordable, reliable, sustainable and modern energy for all.

-Goal 13: Take urgent action to combat climate change and its impacts.

-Goal 14: Conserve and sustainably use the oceans, seas and marine resources for sustainable development.

-Goal 15: Protect, restore and promote sustainable use of terrestrial ecosystems, sustainably manage forests, combat desertification, and halt and reverse land degradation and halt biodiversity loss.

These five goals show clearly how important environmental issues are for the United Nations in general. The recently popular concept of sustainability, which everyone interprets as they wish, is also quite significant.

The question we need to ask here is: who has the right to impose sanctions and penalize countries that do not adhere to the idea of reducing greenhouse gas emissions? From the point of view of international law, no one imposes such penalties. There is no special Climate Change Court to impose penalties. Yes, it is true that in the European Union, fines can be imposed on countries that do not keep their promises. These fines are related to specific pollution of water, soil or air in a given area. This is an example of how a supranational entity can control a single sovereign state.

There are also special carbon quotas in the European Union, which are bought from specific plants for a certain amount (EU emissions trading system). The goal is to reduce greenhouse gas emissions by 55% by 2030 (compared to 1990), and to achieve carbon neutrality by 2050. This amount is then used to deploy green energy technologies across the European Union. The system started operating in 2005 and is the first system of its kind in the world.

Is it possible to achieve such a system worldwide? It would be unfair for many reasons. There are countries with vast deposits of coal and oil. What should these countries do if these resources are banned? Who will rebuild their economy? What to say about the countries using nuclear energy? It is likely that nuclear energy will be banned in the near future. Can we replace it with something else? Probably we cannot. The facts show that green energy CANNOT replace nuclear energy.

It is unfair to force certain countries to switch to green energy. Besides, who controls this? Why does the United Nations ignore what China does? Does China comply with all regulations and treaties? One such coercion would seem to be an economic war, because certain countries will be deprived of much of their resources. The European Union can afford to go green; but the United States and Canada would have serious trouble if they did.

There are people who question entirely such initiatives. They argue that environmental issues are a cover for introducing new business models. Maybe that is true. Those who manage to quickly adapt to the new requirements will be able to get rich quick. But the truth is that green energy alone will not change anything. It all depends on our approach to the world and to other people. Companies like Tesla, for example, boast of being "green," but is that really the case? And does not the UN actually support such businesses? Maybe all this is just a new distribution of wealth around the world!

Of course, we do not want to enter the realm of conspiracy theories. This is not our problem to say who the United Nations work for. The point is that the UN's initiatives are controversial and are unlikely to have much effect. After all, what have the UN achieved of all these Millennium development goals? Child mortality in the Third World remains high, and malaria and AIDS are still here. The idea of sustainability is wonderful, but sustainability is not immeasurable. There are no specific indicators for it to measure it. It is more a matter of hypothesis, of assumptions.

What we call „green business" here is a real phenomenon. It does exist and it really benefits from certain UN initiatives. We cannot prove that all this is done on purpose, but it seems to be purposeful.

2.4 Conclusion

The facts are that the transition to a "green economy" will cost a lot of money to all of us, and that the average taxpayer must be asked what he thinks about it. Such decisions cannot be made at the highest level. The same is true not only of the United States, but of many other countries whose citizens have never been asked about these changes. For example, EU citizens have never given their opinion on the so-called Green Deal that will invest hundreds of billions of euros in renewable energy technologies. Is this what America is expecting? This is very likely. At the same time, China continues to produce greenhouse gases so that it can soon become the world's number one economy.

Of course, the world is moving forward. Science and technology are evolving. We cannot deny the conception of green energy, which in itself is a wonderful idea. The problem is that *we cannot rely on it alone. The decision is to introduce it gradually, and our abandonment of fossil fuels will occur after at least 40-50 years*, when green energy will be enough for us.

Global warming is a fact, but the human influence on it remains unproved scientifically. Such an argument exists only in the minds of radical green activists. They focus only on hot weather and fires, but do not mention the unusually cold weather in Texas in 2021. Whatever happens is the result of global warming! But this is not a science, it is just a dogma defended by a certain group of green activists.

But behind the green ideology there is something else, more frightening. Many of the greens themselves do not realize it. They profess ideas close to communism. We have to analyze what damage communism causes to the environment and why communism will always be in conflict with the heart of green ideology.

Chapter III: Environmentalism and socialism

Contemporary green movements share views close to socialism. They believe that environmental problems today are due to the capitalist economy and the free market. According to them, as we have already seen in our analysis so far, poverty is related to the environment. By solving environmental problems, we must also turn to the economy and move to an entirely new system of economic relations. *We often hear that capitalism is to blame for everything*, and only if we returned to socialism we could save the planet.

Here we will refer to an article by James Plested published on the platform *Capitalism and Environment* in February 2020. The author is obviously affiliated with the left-wing ideology and claims that we need to eradicate capitalism in order to keep our planet clean. The material found in this article is typical of all leftwing environmentalists, thus we can take it as containing universal principles of eco socialism and the Green movements in general.

According to Plested, the presidents of the most developed states support the cause of capitalism. As he observes, "With the likes of Donald Trump, Vladimir Putin and Jair Bolsonaro in charge of some of the world's biggest economies, the prospects for a major shift occurring soon appear terrifyingly dim" (Plested par. 7). These politicians do not take into account the warnings issued by various scientists, and we will suffer due to this ignorance, according to Plested.

As is the case in America, in the words of Plested, "Morrison, Trump and their fellow fossil fuel enthusiasts act not simply in accordance with their personal whims and desires but as the conscious servants of a system: capitalism. Proponents of capitalism talk as if it's the natural form of human society" (Plested par. 8). In short, such persons are paid by big corporations to defend their interests and to resist any environmental taxes or reductions. This opinion is proved with the following words: "The ruling class's lack of concern for the environment is reinforced by the competitive nature of the system. Each individual capitalist must keep their costs low and their profits high to stay ahead of their rivals" (Plested par. 18). Furthermore, we will explain what is "capitalism" and why communism is afraid so much of this system.

James Plested, as well as many other green socialists, believe that the world is ruled by wealthy capitalists and democracy is only a tool in their hands. States support big corporations, and politicians do not think about ordinary people or workers. As he claims, "The role of the capitalist state… is to protect and advance the interests of big business and the rich, rather than the mass of the population who suffer the consequences of their environmentally destructive practices" (Plested par. 21). All that means that any transformation must start with the government and democracy. Capitalists have the power in their hands, so media and educational institutions are on their side. We have to abandon capitalism and "capitalist ideology" and turn to socialism!

Capitalism, as Plested asserts confidently, is something transitional; it will end soon. It is a comparatively new system that exploits people's energy and resources. As he puts it, "If the capitalist system was most befitting of our human nature, you would expect its emergence to have been embraced by all whose lives were transformed by it. But the birth of capitalism in the 17th and 18th centuries was an extremely violent process" (Plested par. 9). This criticism should be taken in a moral aspect, meaning that capitalism is immoral and should be abandoned because of this.

The main “vice” of capitalism is the desire to gain profit. As Plested claims, a capitalist does not care about the environment because the profit is gained in the form of money, not of land; in feudal times, lords were dependent on their land and could not do anything destructive (like to cut forests, etc.). Plested maintains that “If a capitalist destroys their land – say by digging up all the coal or oil it contains, poisoning it with chemicals or exhausting the fertility of the soil through over-farming – they can simply take the profits they’ve generated from it and buy more land elsewhere” (Plested par. 14).

Capitalists, as Plested and many other eco socialists assert, do not care about the environment and are ready to destroy it. By not saving resources, big corporations increase their profits. James Plested claims that “The capitalist class gains immense savings from treating environmental destruction as an ‘externality’ that they can pass on to society” (Plested par. 19). In brief, the so-called capitalists have profit only if they destroy nature or pollute the environment. But we will prove that this assertion is wrong because communist countries have a bad history as regards environmental issues.

From all this we get the impression that green activists are actually socialists. But is it true that green movements and activists are socialists? What does socialism have in common here? We will show that, in fact, *socialism and environmental protection are incompatible*. We will prove this by referring to the theorists of socialism themselves, as well as to the history of socialism and communism in the world. We will give examples of environmental catastrophes and pollution that remain neglected by the communist government.

3.1 Socialism and environmentalism: theoretical connections

Summary:

Here we will discuss what is socialism/communism and what is its theoretical foundation. This analysis is intended only to introduce the reader to Karl Marx's doctrine, not to analyze the whole of it. We will relate this knowledge to what we know about the green movements. The movement called eco socialism will be discussed in the present subchapter.

Socialism and communism are frequently used terms, not only in the field of politics but also of culture, morality, education, and so forth. But there are many misunderstandings when we speak about communism. This is why we need to formulate some definitions here.

To make our analysis clearer, we will define the following concepts here as follows:

1. Socialism - a political movement that believes that the capitalist economy must be transformed in such a way that wealth and resources are distributed equally to all.

2. Communism - a more extreme form of socialism, in which this new distribution is achieved through a bloody revolution. After that, only the workers can have the power and they decide what to do with their resources. Here we will talk about "communist countries", because the power is taken through a revolution in all of them.

3. Eco socialism - an environmental movement based on the ideas of Karl Marx. It argues that we need an "environmental revolution" that will erase inequality and

redistribute resources around the world. This movement is rather socialism than a green movement.

Before going to the history of communist states and their ecological attitudes and issues, we will present the story of the founder of communism (the more radical form of socialism[7]). This person was the German philosopher Karl Marx in the mid-19th century. He began writing in the 1840s. Some of his works were entirely of philosophical nature, and he received a PhD after a work on the materialism of Democritus. Because of his anti-governmental ideas, he fled to Belgium and then to England, where he settled in one of the most industrialized cities in the world, Manchester.

While in Germany, Marx became friends with the son of a manufacturer, Friedrich Engels. Engels proved to be a "sponsor" of Marx's work. Both wrote philosophical works, one of them being *The Capital*- the fundamental work of communism.

Marx's philosophy is complicated and self-contradictions can be easily found in it. Furthermore, it is not clear whether other communists should be called Marxists at all (because they rejected some of his views). Because of this, we have to look closer at Marx's main ideas.

The following views can be attributed to Marx:

[7] Socialism emerged in the beginning of the 19th century. Its initial form was utopian, based on the belief that all people could live together, without having private property (like Robert Owen's communes). Karl Marx criticized this type of socialism and called it "utopian."

1. Ontological materialism - he believed that there are no independent spiritual beings in the world. Everything can be explained by reference to matter, to the material, the corporeal.

2. Greed of the capitalists - according to him, all industrialists and entrepreneurs are greedy and want only to increase their profits at the expense of workers and employees. Thus, they maintain inequality and poverty among the masses.

3. Historical materialism - this is an idea close to the philosophy of Georg Hegel. Marx believed that history is driven by necessity. Everything that happens is necessary, it is not the result of human will or choice. Humanity is evolving so that it passes from one economic stage to another. We are now in a stage of crisis of capitalism, which will soon disintegrate. Therefore, it is time for a revolution that will accelerate this disintegration.

4. Revolution - this is the concept with which communism is most often associated. And this is entirely justified- Marx believed that workers must seize power by force, because now is the time to do so. The right moment should not be missed. Therefore, he said, workers must be enlightened and educated. This means that communist propaganda must turn directly to them and inspire them to carry out a revolution.

5. Dialectics - this is a method created by the ancient Greek philosopher Heraclitus and later developed by Georg Hegel. Dialectics understands the world as composed of opposites. The clash of these opposites leads to development. Thus, capitalists and workers will clash, and this will bring humanity to a new stage of development.

6. Militant atheism- Marx was an opponent of Christianity and religion in general, claiming that it helps the "ruling class" gain control and dominate. This view would be taken later by Vladimir Lenin, one of the ideologues of the demolition of churches in Russia.

7. Internationalism- all workers in the world are one "nation," so they need to unite and fight against their "enemy." National borders should be abolished, and one global communist state founded.

The reader may notice that there is no trace of ecology in all this. The truth is that in the middle of the 19th century such problems did not exist. As we have seen, some American philosophers were aware of the need to communicate with nature and preserve it, but then industrial pollution was not criticized. This criticism did not appear until after the First World War, when environmental problems were already visible to all.

Of course, socialism today is quite different. As early as the beginning of the 20th century, various socialist movements split and even came into conflict with each other. The supporters of the revolution began to call themselves communists. They were led by Vladimir Lenin, who carried out the revolution in Russia. But in Western Europe - especially in Germany, France, and Italy - social democracy appeared, which was a socialist movement against the revolution. It was rather a critique of capitalism. In addition, the collapse of the USSR and the emergence of democracy in Eastern Europe led to the green movements distancing themselves en masse from the ideas of Marx and Lenin. That is why today there are few green activists who speak directly about the revolution. And yet, they exist, as we will see later.

Why should a green activist admire Marx and communism? Because most green movements today are against capitalism. It is true that some people secretly profess Marx's ideas, but they are afraid that they will be criticized. That is why they turn to environmental movements. Of course, not all green supporters are like that. But *they basically stick to the green ideology because of the critique of capitalism.* This is one of the fundamental theses of all green movements in the world - capitalism must be reformed, and even abolished.

Do the Greens themselves realize how wrong this adherence to socialism is? In fact, some of them are even proud of it. They believe that socialism is the only salvation from all the problems we have today. Left movements gained momentum in the last years after the crisis of 2008. Then the banking system shook, which had negative consequences for people's confidence in the system. The Occupy Wallstreet movement emerged, which was something of a protest against the modern form of capitalism. This movement faded and disappeared, but it is a fact that left-wing ideas are trendy today.

When we speak of the "left," we mean moderate socialism or social democracy, not communism in its Stalinist or Maoist form. In this sense, green activists have found an important connection that inspires them. Yes, most of them probably have not read Marx; most do not want to carry out a revolution. And yet, they are influenced by Marx through various intermediaries, i.e. philosophers who interpret Marx's ideas and disseminate them as their own.

Obviously, it is difficult to put all green activists under one definition. The green movements, as we have noted, are diverse, and we cannot say that they are all Marxists.

But certainly the big green NGOs, as well as other organizations, share the ideas of socialism, even if they are not aware of it.

And yet, what the green movements offer today is a new kind of socialism. It is not based on the idea of legal equality or revolution. However, this new kind of socialism speaks of the transformation of the "system", of the abolition of capitalist economic relations; it criticizes consumerism and globalization. The idea of a "circular economy" is also very important here - what is produced should not be thrown away. We need to make as little waste as possible and use cheaper materials. Thus, all products will be easily accessible to different people, regardless of their social status. To this, we must add more affordable means of transportation, as well as avoiding air travel (because it pollutes the environment more than all other means of transportation).

The last of these things have nothing to do with Marxism. However, they are based on the Marxist attitude, which seeks equal distribution of all resources and wants to prevent individuals from getting rich. If we all use cheap and old clothes, many people will not be able to accumulate wealth, but what is worse is that unemployment will increase. And here we see another contradiction among the green movements: *there is no way to provide work for everyone and produce less at the same time*. The only solution here would be for all people to be involved in agriculture alone, but that will take us far back in technological terms.

We will now turn to the ideas of a supporter of eco socialism, or the current that wants to link the socialist revolution with the ecological revolution. John Bellamy Foster, who is a researcher in the field of economy and environment, points out that "Historically, however, socialism has influenced the development of ecological thought and practice, while ecology has informed socialist thought and practice. Since the nineteenth century, the relationship between the two has been complex, interdependent, and dialectical" (Foster 1).

The word "dialectical" here means that man and nature are in a relationship of contradiction. They are in constant conflict, and yet they exist in unity. In this sense, eco socialism does not fully correspond to Marxism, because eco socialism sees the relationship between man and nature as harmonious. Dialectics, on the other hand, denies harmony. It focuses more on conflict and confrontation.

Foster says we are facing more than an environmental catastrophe. We have to make a decision because we do not have much time. As he states, "We can continue on the path of business as usual and risk catastrophic Earth-system change… or we can take the transformative route of social-system change aimed at egalitarian human development in coevolution with the vital parameters of the earth" (Foster 2). All this means that we can only be saved by abolishing the current economic and social system. In short, we must say goodbye to capitalism!

But did Marx foresee a similar ecological catastrophe in the future? According to Foster, environmental ideas can be found in Marx. For example, he talks about the connection between the social and the natural, about the fact that there is a certain "metabolism" in nature and in society. As Foster notes, "Marx's concepts of the universal metabolism of nature, the social metabolism, and the metabolic rift have proven invaluable for modeling the complex relation between social-productive systems ... and the larger ecological systems" (Foster 4). Foster thus claims that nature and society exist in a relation of mutual dependency.

In fact, this concept found in Marx has little to do with modern ecology. As mentioned, in the 19th century, environmental issues were rarely raised and addressed. Marx's conception of the human-nature relationship is important insofar as it affirms the need for conflict between these two entities. Man governs nature, and at the same time he is part of it, i.e. follows its laws. Let us not forget that Karl Marx was also influenced by Charles Darwin and considered man to be a being entirely belonging to the material world.

Another supposedly ecological idea that can be found in Marx is the connection between capitalism and the deprivation of resources. As Foster argues, "A distinctive characteristic of Marxian ecological theory has been an emphasis on unequal ecological exchange, or ecological imperialism, in which it is understood that one country can ecologically exploit another." Such an example is given with England, which exported soil from Ireland (Foster 7). But this is all that can be found in Marx's philosophy and has something to do with ecology.

In fact, Marx's views of revolution, as well as his critique of capitalism, had the strongest influence on modern Greens. It is no coincidence that this supporter of eco-socialism says that "What is required, then, is an ecological and social revolution that will facilitate a society of ecological sustainability and substantive equality" (Foster 8). Foster is an example of how far a green activist can go!

As Foster goes on to say, we can only deal with climate change by changing the "system." He notes that "The ecosocialist movement has adopted the slogan System Change Not Climate Change, but a capitalist system deeply entrenched worldwide infuses the current omnipresent reality." However, as he goes on, "The dominance of the capitalist mode of production means that revolutionary change on the scale needed to confront the planetary environmental emergency remains beyond the immediate social horizon" (Foster 8). He wants to say that people think rather about their physical survival (because of poverty) than about environmental issues.

In short, such a revolution is difficult to carry out today because the conditions are not in place for it to emerge. More people need to be aware of the planet's environmental problems and respond, but this will only happen when they are threatened by poverty, hunger and even extinction from the planet itself. Most likely, such riots will become more frequent in the future, among young people (now). As Foster writes, "Since the challenge of maintaining a resilient earth will face the younger generations the most, we can expect that youth will become disenchanted and radicalized as the material conditions of existence deteriorate" (Foster 10). So, if poverty increases, this will increase the chance for young people to rebel against "the system."

Here comes the idea of a future revolution similar to that in Russia in 1917. Since the proletariat no longer exists in the old, classical sense of the word, something that the author calls the "ecological proletariat" will appear. As he argues, "In the not-too-distant future, an 'environmental proletariat'—signs of which are already present — will almost inevitably emerge from the combination of ecological degradation and economic hardship, particularly at the bottom of society" (Foster 10). These will be people affected by climate change and the various disasters associated with it. As we saw in previous chapters of this book, some green alarmists believe that the world is moving toward impoverishment, although the facts show otherwise. They predict future crises that will be due to global warming and the expected rise in ocean levels. This will lead to protests and attempts by the "eco proletariat" to take power into its own hands.

But eco socialism itself is not a homogeneous doctrine. There are internal currents in it that differ from each other. In the 1970s, for example, there were green movements that were very critical of Marx and socialism. For example, eco socialists Ted Benton and Andre Gorz "employed the new ecology of Green theory to criticize Marx for allegedly failing to address issues of sustainability" (Foster 5). This is due to what was happening in Eastern Europe and the Soviet Union, as well as criticism from the Frankfurt School[8].

This may seem strange today, but environmental movements have not always been on the side of socialism, or at least Stalin's type of socialism. As we will show later, in the former communist countries, the green movements distance themselves from socialism. *Ergo*, it is not true that green movements are inspired ONLY by socialism or by Marx. But there is such connection in the United States, and this evident fact cannot be denied.

Later, however, the Greens began to turn to Marx and realize that their path was parallel to socialism. An entirely positive attitude toward Marx emerged in the 1990s. As Foster writes, "The hybrid approach changed in the late 1990s when others, most notably Paul Burkett, demonstrated the deep ecological context in which Marx's original critique had been constructed." This was rather an attempt to see environmentalism in Marx's philosophy, but according to the author, it was successful. However, the truth is that one can find in Mar anything one wants; but true ecological philosophy or attitude is missing in his works.

---

[8] A Leftist school in philosophy that was founded in the German city of Frankfurt. It criticized Stalinism and the idea of a violent revolution. However, it spread ideas that today we call "cultural Marxism."

As Foster claims that "The new analysis included the systematic reconstruction of Marx's argument on social metabolism. The result was the development of important Marxian ecological concepts, together with a reunification of Marxian theory" (Foster 5). In short, eco-socialism has recently adhered to Marxism and argued that only in Marx can we find the right solution to the ecological crisis.

In conclusion, we can say that Marxism, as well as its interpretations by left-wing philosophers (such as the representatives of the Frankfurt School) have a serious influence on the concept of modern green movements. Eco socialism is only a branch of the green movements; this means that its members are not ashamed to admit that they are socialists. Other green activists prefer not to be called that because they think "politics is a dirty thing." At the same time, they are dealing precisely with politics!

Without participation in politics, modern green movements would be unpopular and have little influence over social and economic processes. Although they present themselves and define themselves as "active citizens," there is a lot of politics in them, and they prefer to be represented in Congress as much as possible. It is obvious that they are inclined to the ideas of the Liberal Party, so we can find such green activists in its ranks.

We mentioned that the eco socialists are opposed to globalization. What is the reason for this? We know from Marx's doctrine that borders are not considered real and that all nations must live in unity (this is the so-called internationalism). Globalization, according to left-wing philosophers, does not conform to the principle of internationalism. In fact, it enables large corporations to do business anywhere in the world and control a growing share of the world's markets. This control in turn means that corporations are not interested in solving both poverty and the environmental problems of a country. They offer lower-than-normal salaries to citizens of Third World countries. They offer worse working conditions than, for example, in the United States. For this reason, green movements oppose globalization as a means of enriching certain corporations and a small circle of individuals. According to the Greens, corporations must bear their responsibility for environmental pollution and other environmental problems, and they should pay a special "green tax."

There is some truth in all this, but it is not entirely true. Thanks to globalization, the green movements themselves can easily spread their ideas and connect with other organizations. They organize international actions (such as Greta Thunberg's "Global climate strike"), which is entirely due to globalization. In addition, large corporations employ tens of millions of people around the world, and their collapse would lead to huge unemployment. In short, green movements have no understanding of economics and should not deal with economic issues!

In fact, *socialism/communism has done a great deal of damage to humanity, including in the field of ecology*. Green activists need to read more about this and realize that socialism is not the way to save our planet. We will now turn to this and see what has happened to the communist countries in Europe and around the world, as well as what is happening now in communist China.

3.2 Communism: A history of environmental disasters

Summary:

The history of communist states shows that they neglected environmental issues and even created new ones. Pollution and contamination were inevitable for the communist economy. Here we will discuss some ecological issues that emerged in Eastern Europe during the period of Communist regimes and the Chernobyl tragedy in the Soviet Union.

Green activists often argue that environmental crises stem from capitalism and industrialization. According to them, large corporations tend to pollute more, because only in such a manner can they reduce their losses. But as we will see here, the facts say otherwise. *Countries that have adopted communism as their ideology are failing completely in environmental terms*. Moreover, they are becoming the most polluted countries in the world, which in some cases (Chernobyl) turns out to be disastrous even for the Western world.

Communism as an ideology aims at rapid industrial development, in view of the idea of creating a powerful communist state that would overtake the "capitalist" countries. This seems absurd - why would a person fighting against capitalism want such a rapid industrialization? Because most countries that accept communism as their doctrine were agricultural, with underdeveloped industries. That is why it was very important for them to catch up with their Western competitors. Moreover, Marx believed that capitalism cannot simply be "erased" from our planet. It must be brought to its logical end. This will happen as workers take control of all factories (or in modern terms, all corporations).

The rapid industrialization and development of technology were to make the communist countries leaders in the world economy. To this end, communist governments removed all restrictions on this development. Ecology turned out to be unnecessary, and it was argued that only in Western countries there are environmental problems.

Rapid industrialization led to huge pollution of water, air and soil in Eastern Europe, the USSR, China and other countries. As the researcher Bohdana Kurylo observes, "there was the state's uncontrollable desire to display its power through the advancement of Soviet technology and society, leading to chaotic achievements at the expense of the unprepared and underdeveloped society" (Kurylo 58). The only goal was to build a huge number of factories, as well as the production of a certain number of products (all this was determined by a 5-year plan). Everything else remained in the background. What are the working conditions, what is the pay, what happens with the industrial waste - these are questions that were not asked in the countries subject to the ideology of communism.

Interestingly, the Chernobyl nuclear accident on April 26, 1986 was the first case in which communist industry began to be criticized that it harmed nature. Then communist rulers began to pay attention to environmental issues because society became too distrustful of the government. As Kurylo puts it, "Until the Chernobyl catastrophe, environmental problems were only attributed to the nature of the American capitalist system that prioritized profits over its citizens, which seemed to have been impossible in socialist society" (Kurylo 61). But it turned out that "the American system" is much better because it prevents such accidents (although it has been close to it several times).

In an article from 2001, the researcher David Turnock exposes his research on the history of environmental issues brought about by communism. According to him, *we can find many examples of environmental catastrophes caused by poor communist governance*. Green activists today would be shocked to learn about the ecological conditions in Eastern Europe under communism. *The history of communism is in fact a history of pollution and enormous damage to nature*. As he writes, "Pollution was reaching unacceptable levels by the 1980s, after years of rapid growth combined with a dismissive ideological stance associating pollution only with capitalism, which delayed serious consideration of the problem" (Turnock 485). He gives the example of huge pollution in East Germany, Czechoslovakia, Poland and Romania. In these countries, factories operated around the clock, harmful raw materials were used, and nothing to prevent the pollution of air, water and soil. As this researcher notes, "The most serious environmental problems concerning air and water pollution impacting human health as well as the physical environment" (Turnock 485). Examples of pollution were heavy smog, air contamination, water pollution in every communist country in Europe. There was no country ruled by the Communists that was not spared these problems.

Smog in the big cities in these countries was a normal thing. For example, in Prague, the capital of Czechoslovakia, in the 1980s there was smog all winter. In some parts of Poland there was smog even in summer. Coal was widely used in Czechoslovakia, East Germany and Poland. As Turnock writes, "In 1989 two thirds of thermal electricity in Czechoslovakia came from brown coal with high sulfur and ash content… The fallout gave rise to smog problems in Prague and northern Bohemia during the winter" (Turnock 485).

But it is not just big cities that suffered from these problems. This observation also applies to small towns and villages. Turnock observes the following: "The rural areas did not escape ... Heavy metals, associated with mining activities, are often present in the soil: Around Eisleben in East Germany… there are concentrations of arsenic, cadmium and zinc" (Turnock 486). These are extremely dangerous elements that should not be trapped in the atmosphere or water. Unfortunately, communist governments did not talk about this at all, but had to keep it quiet. Citizens also did not touch on this topic because they could be subjected to repression.

As the author mentions, environmental movements did not appear until the mid-1980s, when Perestroika (an attempt to reform communism) was already beginning. Their protests remained small and were not attended by many people, because a large part of the population worked in factories that polluted nature.

But all this pollution had other effects. It led to a worse standard of living, the flight of animal species, as well as problems with water and agriculture. David Turnock states that "Pollution was in many respects counterproductive leading not only to environmental problems but also to wasted resources. This impacted on the economy in many ways. Farm and timber yields were reduced while fish stocks declined" (Turnock 487). Farmers, as well as fishing, suffered from the rapid industrialization. But all this was not talked about, because industrial development should not be hindered.

Apart from Czechoslovakia and East Germany, another serious example of pollution is the Silesian region of Poland. This is one of the largest coal basins in the world. Also, during communism, many people found work there. This job was also highly paid because it is challenging. As Turnock mentions, "In Poland 13 mln people inhabited ecologically contaminated areas, including Upper Silesia where very high sulfur dioxide concentrations caused serious health problems" (Turnock 488). Poland used only coal at that time to produce electricity (just like Czechoslovakia, currently Poland has not built a nuclear power plant).

Unfortunately, the historical landmarks in these areas also have suffered from all this. Big cities like Prague, Krakow, Warsaw, have been severely affected by dust particles and smog. As Turnock writes, "The effects of pollution on the urban fabric were particularly regrettable in historic cities like Krakow and Prague. Despite the scheduling of protected areas… there could be no defense against the debilitating effects of pollution as buildings were literally eaten away" (Turnock 488). Governments guided by the principles of communism were not interested in beautiful architecture or the need to preserve these landmarks. Such pollution has had a detrimental effect on the centers of large cities, forcing people to move from there because of the bad quality of air and the inability to go out even for a normal walk.

Some researchers ask whether there is a link between environmental problems and the collapse of the Soviet Union and its satellites. As we will see later, such a connection maybe exists. According to David Turnock, there was a deep crisis in the 1980s that affected these regimes. He states that "It is now well-established that environmental problems encountered at this time amounted to a crisis which had a significant bearing on the chain of revolutions paving the way for the current transition" (Turnock 489).

Of course, we cannot say for sure that it was the careless attitude towards ecology that shattered the regimes in Eastern Europe and the USSR. A much more logical explanation is President Reagan's tough policy and the Soviet Union's inability to compete in the armed race. Also, in the 1980s, many economic problems arose, which showed that the end of this system was near.

It is curious to note that after 1984-5, a few green organizations appeared. They were informal and could not participate in the politics of these countries. In the Soviet Union, even a branch of Greenpeace appeared, but it worked for too short a time. Green activists in Eastern Europe were a kind of opposition, and they criticized the government for its inability to deal with environmental crises. In addition to the pollution that we mentioned, these movements were organized after the Chernobyl nuclear accident in contemporary Ukraine, which was part of the Soviet Union at that time. This was an event that was hidden from the authorities in the USSR for a week, but eventually people found out about it from foreign radio stations.

It was Chernobyl that led to a massive collapse in confidence in the communist government. In addition, Chernobyl led to a boom in green movements. After it, the topic of ecology was no longer taboo in these countries. It was discussed very seriously in politics and the government was forced to take action against pollution.

The so-called transition to democracy and free-market economy in postcommunist countries was beneficial to them. As Turnock notes, the transformation of communist/socialist economy into market economy "has been considered generally advantageous for the environment because the region's resource endowment is not suited to heavy industry and market driven restructuring has increased the role of services which are generally less polluting" (Turnock 490). The market economy is able to care more about nature and the environment, and the former communist countries are proof of that.

As the author notes with facts, today these countries are less polluted and hardly anyone would go back to the times when the big cities in Poland, Czechoslovakia and East Germany were covered by smog. This example demonstrates that communism pollutes, and democracy and "capitalism" have to correct the mistakes of the communist rapid industrialization.

Regarding this transition and improvement, Turnock reports that "In the Czech Republic as a whole there have been reductions in carbon dioxide, sulfur dioxide and - more substantially - in the production and consumption of ozone depleting gases. Decreased lignite consumption means lower pollution levels in the mining area " (Turnock 491). The market economy has led these countries to use resources and technologies that spare nature more. If the theory of the eco socialists was true, then Eastern Europe would have been more polluted today than it was before 1989. But the facts say the opposite- *these countries are now cleaner in comparison with the times of communism*! *Communist industries pollute a lot*, and this is a fact.

Undoubtedly, the most significant environmental disaster of the 1980s was Chernobyl. Not much is known about this catastrophe in America. What we do know is mostly based on the show of the same name broadcast on HBO. Here are some facts related to it:

During a safety inspection on April 26, 1986, one of the reactors at the Chernobyl nuclear power plant refused to operate properly. After a while, the employees realized that there is a radiation leak. It was believed that this is a small leakage, which had already occurred several times in other power plants. At first, the approach to the problem was frivolous and careless. Although the fire brigade was called, as well as medical teams, the authorities did not announce anything to the population. Residents of a small town (with about 50 000 inhabitants) nearby were not evacuated until the next day. During this time, they were exposed to a considerable amount of radiation. Dozens of people, including firefighters and medics, died or were sent to hospital in a fatal condition.

The people of the USSR were then completely cut off from the world and could not listen to Western radio stations. They also did not have the opportunity to watch Western television. While in Poland, Czechoslovakia and East Germany citizens already had some information, those in the USSR relied entirely on their rulers, the Communist Party of the Soviet Union. A large parade was organized on the occasion of one of the communist holidays on May 1. A few days later, the leader of the USSR, Mikhail Gorbachev, was forced to admit that there was an accident at the Chernobyl nuclear power plant and that there was a radiation leak. However, he did not mention the size of the accident and the fact that the population of several republics within the USSR was endangered. Immediate measures were not taken, such as shutting the factories and ordering everyone to stay at home. Timely analysis of radiation contained in air, soil and water was not performed.

Communism does not care about nature; but it also ignores the health of its citizens. According to the young Ukrainian researcher Bohdana Kurylo, the problem of the communist government is the following: “The USSR’s domestic failure laid in the reluctance to prioritize the wellbeing of its citizens. It was sharply highlighted in the immediate aftermath of the accident. Firefighters ... were not aware of the radiation and lacked relevant clothing and equipment” (Kurylo 57). As already mentioned, it was more important to develop industry and production, and to eliminate radical social division[9]. The Soviet government even wanted to build as many nuclear power plants as possible in order to provide the necessary energy for all this production.

But the government did this at the cost of many human lives. As Kurylo points out, "The Soviet government failed to construct a safe nuclear power station, disregarding the problems concerning its operation and neglecting to prevent the fallout from causing further damage." Important information was hidden from the citizens after the catastrophe and this led to the disappearance of trust in the government of the USSR: "Knowing their faults, the Politburo tried to contain the truth from people, further alienating them" (Kurylo 59).

The psychological dimensions of this catastrophe are not to be underestimated. These damages were much stronger than the damage to human health. After this catastrophe, the people of Ukraine began to live in insecurity. They thought: What will happen if a nuclear accident takes place again? Are Soviet nuclear plants safe? As Kurylo reports, "For the majority of the post-Soviet citizens, especially in Ukraine, Chernobyl will be forever remembered as a personal tragedy and the point of no return to what had seemed certain" (Kurylo 66). For us this is simply a TV show; but for many people in Eastern Europe, it is a personal tragedy- some people lost their friends or relatives due to radiation.

The real problem of Chernobyl has been the people's fear that all this may happen again and that the government will not help them, not warn them. Since then, in the

---

[9] Social equality was achieved in Communist countries, but actually it prevented the citizens from the opportunity to become wealthier. Their salaries and incomes were similar, and the citizens could afford to buy cheap things, but not good cars or other equipment.

former communist countries, there has been a huge distrust of the government and scepticism to any information coming from it. The level of distrust is the same even today.

The economic damage from Chernobyl was also a huge blow for the USSR. This tragedy put an end to the idea of a powerful USSR with vast energy resources. The construction of new nuclear power plants stopped, unlike in the Western world, where nuclear power plants were built, with an emphasis on safety. Such a tragedy can happen anywhere, but only in the USSR was such information concealed- unlike the crisis in Japan in 2011, when one of their largest nuclear power plants was hit by an earthquake.

As Kurylo notes, "Technologically, the USSR was behind even the newly industrialized countries of Asia, where Chernobyl's consequences drained a huge amount of money from the economy. Socially, the Chernobyl tragedy awoke public discontent" (Kurylo 64). The dream of a powerful Soviet Union was over. The end was near and the citizens felt it.

Bohdana Kurylo has his own point of view on whether Chernobyl led to the collapse of the Soviet Union. She states that "despite the temptation to claim Chernobyl to be the sole reason for the failure of the Soviet citizens' belief in their state, as well as the fall of the Soviet Union, it would be an oversimplified misjudgment, as Chernobyl was a trigger but not the cause." As she goes on, "Its major role was in highlighting the systematic failures of the government, and more importantly, the failure to establish trust between the government and the people of the USSR" (Kurylo 55). The citizens realized that they were deceived by the communist leaders.

It is interesting that after that disaster, green movements appeared in the Soviet Union. However, as absurd as this may be, they were linked to nationalism. To understand this, we must keep in mind that the USSR consisted of many republics and nations. These peoples wanted independence in the late 1980s, and the green movements were associated with the doctrine of the sovereign nation-state. As Kurylo writes, "While environmentalism around the globe tended to be characterized by its 'one world' outlook, environmentalists in the USSR blamed the central government for environmental issues and sought to address them by taking control over their regions" (Kurylo 65). In short, green movements in communist countries were fundamentally different from modern environmental movements. This means that *not all green activists follow the same ideology*. Differences are possible due to the specific political history of the given country.

Everything we have listed so far shows perfectly well that the green movements are wrong in adhering to socialism. In fact, they have to run right away from it. Maybe *American green organizations should communicate more with their colleagues from former communist countries*. In this way, *they will understand how much they are wrong, relying on the ideas of Karl Marx and other left-wing philosophers*.

One might say that the communist countries are an example of forced and premature industrialization, and that the problem is precisely the availability of factories. If we resign from building factories and producing more and more, then we will not pollute the planet. This is not an illogical conclusion, but then unemployment and poverty will increase and our civilization will go back by centuries. Is that what our green movements want? It is doubtful that they would want precisely that.

The crisis caused by the rapid industrialization of the Soviet Union and its satellites was due to negligence about environmental problems, and about the wellbeing of ordinary people in general. Do socialism or communism in essence contradict green ideas? The answer is affirmative. Perhaps the Greens themselves are aware of this fact and that is why they do not so passionately defend socialism. This is evidenced by the very fact that there is a movement called "eco socialism." This means that there are also green organizations that do not consider themselves socialist or are not associated with socialism.

All this means that the western system, or the so-called market economy, proves to be a better protector of nature. We can do another analysis that proves exactly that. Let us now turn to communist China, which is the world leader in polluting our planet.

3.3 The biggest polluter on Earth

Summary:

In spite of all measures taken by international organizations and the richest countries in the world, environmental problems are mainly caused by China, which is the biggest polluter on our planet. What stands behind this strategy of China? Why does it not abandon fossil fuels? We will see that communist ideology is one of the reasons for this.

By now, we have talked about communism historically, as something that has already happened and is over. Most communist countries are already democratic, they have a market economy. However, there are several countries in the world that still officially adhere to the doctrine of communism. These are China, Cuba and North Korea.

China is a bit of a strange case. In the last 20 years, China has introduced a market economy and opened its doors to Western investments. Many companies have emerged that are developing independently of the state, without state subsidies. All that is required of them is not to sponsor movements that stand against the Communist Party. In practice, the Chinese economy is a mixture of a planned (communist) economy and a free market. The truth is that *China is still ruled by communists*, and we must always keep that in mind when talking to its representatives.

What is happening to the environment in China? We read every day about the smog that has engulfed Beijing; we read about polluted Shanghai, which is among the largest cities in the world. We know that there are many thermal power plants in China and that a lot of coal is used there for energy. Green technologies are gradually being introduced in China, and China is currently trying to show that it is a "green country." But this is not true! *China is another example of a communist country that pollutes nature and does not want to take responsibility* for it.

We will now refer to an article by Richard Smith published in *Foreign Policy* in 2020. In this article, the author proves that China is very far from the idea of nature conservation. This is due entirely to the Communist Party, which has ruled it for over 70 years. As Smith puts it, "The party has often sacrificed environmental regulations as soon as GDP targets and economic growth have been threatened, thus paradoxically producing soaring pollution." But this pollution is not only due to the desire to achieve certain standards or goals. As Smith continues, "Even in normal times, China's soaring carbon dioxide (CO2) emissions are a massive part of the dire threat to all life on earth posed by climate change" (Smith par. 1). In short, no matter how developed China is, it will never turn entirely to environmental solutions. At least that's what Richard Smith believes.

There is one interesting fact: in 1990, China's greenhouse gases emissions were half of those of the United States. In 2017, they were two times more than U.S. emissions (Smith par. 3). Thus, we can understand what is the reason for China's economic growth- the use of cheap energy, no desire to protect the environment, the construction of new plants. At the same time, many Western companies are investing in China and have their factories there! They want to have lower costs, without realizing that this leads to massive pollution on our planet.

But the facts about China are not exhausted with that. As Richard Smith explains, "As the world's largest emitter, accounting for 30 percent of total global emissions against 15 percent for the United States, 9 percent for the EU-28, 7 percent for India, 5 percent for Russia ... China is by far the leading driver of global warming" (Smith par. 9). This is a huge difference - the second largest economy in the world emits as much carbon as the U.S., the EU, and Russia at once! It is true that China's population outnumbers them all - the total population of the United States, the European Union and Russia is about 1 billion, while China's population is 1.4 billion. But this is no excuse because the majority of this population actually lives in poverty, unlike the citizens of the United States and the European Union.

China is trying to recover from the crisis that began in 2020 by giving up green energy. As Richard Smith notes, "Instead of prioritizing clean energy, Xi's government is slashing funding for wind and solar power while ramping up spending on new coal-fired power plants." As he explains, "That's an inevitable result not only of the post-pandemic economic crisis but of the general slowing in the Chinese economy in the last few years" (Smith par. 12).

But all this again cannot explain why the Chinese are polluting so much! It is best to turn to the history of the Soviet Union and see our analysis of the events surrounding the Chernobyl disaster. As this researcher states, "As a state-based ruling class and communist nation in a world dominated by more advanced and powerful capitalist nations, Mao and his successors understood, like the Soviet Union, that they must 'catch up and overtake the United States'." That is, China has to "build relatively self-sufficient high tech superpower economies shielded from Western takeover by barring foreign investment in key state sectors" (Smith par. 16). A powerful and energy-independent communist state will be able to sustain a strong army. But energy resources come first, as does increasing production capacity.

To understand what the Chinese think, we need to make a comparison with the Soviet Union during the Cold War. The USSR's ambitions were to dominate economically and militarily. However, because it could not overtake the United States economically, the Soviet Union decided to rely on military force. Due to this, even after the end of the Cold War, Russia is still a serious rival. Although a poor country, Russia is threatening us with its military might.

However, China does not want to repeat Russia's mistake. It does not want to risk disintegration (because China consists of a number of autonomous territories that would eventually want to become independent states). Also, China intends to build a strong economy first, and at the same time a strong army. Knowing the strength of Western countries, China prefers (and this is quite obvious) not to come into conflict with them. That is why China is now pretending to be open, ready for reforms and interaction with the West.

It is true that China aims to dominate, but this will happen in the long run. China is patient and will slowly achieve its goal. That is why it sacrifices the environment and the health of its citizens. But all this is exacerbating climate change. We have shown that things are not as scary as the green alarms suggest. And yet, we cannot allow just one country to pollute almost the entire planet without being sanctioned! This is not right and it is not fair as well. Why do we need to introduce green technologies and shut down our nuclear power plants, and China can safely use coal without sanctions at the same time?

Climate change is a fact; we still do not know to what extent people are responsible for it. But soil, air and water pollution is something that will have an effect for centuries to come. Even after a possible disintegration of China, the people who will inhabit its territory will suffer from it.

As Richard Smith states, "Environmental concerns come a far second behind the fear of economically induced collapse" (Smith par. 16). He notes that today Chinese citizens are a little richer and that some of them live well. This is so especially in big cities. The Chinese are already used to comfort and do not want to deprive themselves of it. As the author writes, "after centuries of privation and decades of Maoist austerity, China's masses were overdue for some creature comforts." But Smith warns that "the promotion of mindless consumerism for the sake of consumerism on the model of Western capitalism is contributing mightily to China's and the world's waste and pollution crises" (Smith par. 20).

It is clear here that the author is also a critic of Western consumerism, and perhaps of fossil fuels. From this point of view, he also criticizes China and its negligence on environmental issues. It is important for us here to note the fact that communism cannot deal with these problems. The advantage of the Western world is precisely the opportunity to impose new technologies that spare nature and do not harm health. In addition, consumerism in America and Europe is severely limited. People are aware that they need to protect nature and produce less waste, as well as save resources as much as possible.

One might say that China is simply lagging behind in its development and will also reach the point where it will introduce green technologies. Our answer is: it does not matter when China reaches that point in time. The world must act together and solve environmental problems together. Certain countries cannot be excluded from international treaties just because they are "developing countries." Is China really a "developing country"? When will it become a developed country and take on its responsibilities and obligations? As Smith notes, "The problem with all of this is that to maximize economic growth, employment, and consumerism, China's leaders have no choice but to let the polluters pollute. There's just no way around that" (Smith par. 21).

Can we say that China is threatening us in environmental terms? Yes, the answer to this question must be yes. Excessive use of fossil fuels in China will have different effects, but they will certainly spread around the world. It is possible that all this will have an effect on climate change. But the most critical problem is that almost the entire production of machines, cars, etc. has been relocated to China. Thanks to the fact that it does not pay any environmental taxes, China has the opportunity to develop its economy and take our jobs. But there are no protesters there, because there simply cannot be any. As the author says about strict censorship in China, "Given the Great Firewall, most Chinese people today have no idea that their country leads the world in CO2 emissions, and even if they did know, they have no legal means to organize and resist the vainglorious but eco-suicidal ambitions of their rulers" (Smith par. 27). Green movements cannot arise in China because it would be a form of protest; and if they are subordinate to the Communist Party, they simply will not be authentic green movements.

In conclusion, Richard Smith argues that "What's uniquely dangerous about the Chinese case is that its emissions are so huge ... and growing so fast that scientists tell us they could eventually doom the climate on their own regardless of what the rest of the world does" (Smith par. 23). In short, if fossil fuels are actually damaging the atmosphere, China must stop emitting them as soon as possible. In fact, if China does not join international agreements to reduce greenhouse gases, then all these agreements will not make sense! The parties to these contracts will incur huge costs without any effect. This will be a pointless sacrifice.

In addition, we must support countries such as Japan and South Korea, which are our economic and military partners. The pollution that China is causing is reaching these countries. China pollutes seawater as well as air. Japan and South Korea have very different approaches to the environment. They do not give up fossil fuels altogether, but they prefer innovation because they know that the success of the future lies in it. He who controls energy will dominate the world. If you have secure and inexhaustible sources of energy, as well as technologies that work with them, you will dominate. That is why it is important to develop so-called green technologies. But that does not mean that we have to give up the nuclear power plant - something Japan did not do even after the horrific Fukushima accident in 2011.

3.4 Conclusion

Green ideologues today claim that capitalism is to blame for all disasters and nature pollution. According to them, if there was no capitalism, there would be no such disasters. Capitalism alone is to blame for global warming and climate problems. That is why we must switch to a new economic system that abolishes capitalist relations.

Green activists are very naïve in this regard. They need to know more real facts about the communist regimes in the past. The sad thing is that they do not pay much attention to history. According to them, history is written by the "capitalists" and we must have doubts about the facts presented in it.

The Western market economy is without any competition in terms of solving environmental problems. In the United States and Europe, these issues are being talked about openly and real action is being taken. Green organizations operate without any restrictions. No one is chasing them, no one is covering them up. At the same time, they criticize and even want to destroy the system that has helped them for so long!

What about Greta Thunberg, who demonstratively does not go to school, but has the time to travel on a yacht from Europe to New York? When she was 15, she began her "climate strike." Is it right for a girl of that age to give up the free services that the state (in her case, Sweden) provides her? Does Thunberg realize that it is capitalism that allows her to express her opinion freely and point the finger at those she believes are to blame for climate change? And why did not Thunberg go to China to point the finger at the Communist Party?

But Thunberg is given as an example of an "active" young girl who is able to formulate her own claims regarding the environment. She can teach us how to treat nature and how to live without damaging the environment. At the same time, we do not hear too often about China, India or Brazil, some of the biggest polluters on our planet. Why does Thunberg criticize the United States and Western Europe? Why does she not look east, to Russia or China?

The truth is that the modern market economy creates some environmental problems. But any industrial system will create such. We cannot go back by four or five centuries to reduce environmental pollution! We need to look for technological solutions that help in this aspect.

Saying that the market economy is the only system in which we can hope to solve environmental problems honestly and effectively, *we are not saying that we should adhere to the principles of consumerism and even hedonism* (seeking pleasure in everything). Hedonism is one of the causes of the current environmental crisis, as we will see in the last chapter. Nonetheless, there is another solution that can help reduce pollution and change our attitude towards nature without turning to communism. What is this solution, we will see in the next chapter.

Chapter IV: The Christian understanding of the environment and ecology

So far, we have briefly looked at different ideas and theories elaborated by the green movements around the world. Our analysis has been brief, but it presents all the important points in the theories of the greens. By now, we have seen that green movements are diverse, but they still have a slight tendency to prefer socialism; although this contradicts the ecological history of socialism/communism. We have seen that global warming may not be induced by humans, and that it is more appropriate to talk about climate change. We have seen that international conventions often exclude major polluters and that a country like China goes unpunished for polluting a vast area.

But there is another problem here that is often overlooked. Do only green movements have the right to talk about nature conservation? Is this just their exclusive privilege? In this chapter we will talk about an alternative approach to environmental issues. We will show that religion, and Christianity in particular, does not contradict the view of protecting the environment. Our "liberals" think the opposite, but this is a huge mistake. Christians must also think about the environment and protect it, but without leading to radical alarmism or socialism.

4.1 Christianity encourages environment protection

Summary:

There is one incorrect thesis claiming that devastation of nature is rooted in the Christian worldview. It is claimed that in the Book of *Genesis* it is written that man should dominate over all creatures. We will prove that this thesis is wrong because the Bible claims the opposite- that man is not the Lord, and that we have to obey God. There is a solution based on the Christian worldview and we will expose it here.

There was a time when green movements embraced the more educated, wealthier people in society. At that time, not all citizens were interested in this phenomenon. But now environmental issues are everywhere - children start learning about it as children; it is present in the media, in the movies, in the culture. We often see protests and demonstrations in defense of a particular environmental cause.

Citizens of the United States have the feeling that the environment is also involved in decades of "cultural wars." President Trump has often been accused of serving the interests of fossil fuel corporations. The Republican Party has been accused of doing nothing against global warming and even denying it. Even the politician Al Gore based his 2000 campaign on environmental issues and presented his pessimistic scenario for a future environmental catastrophe due to human activity.

Everything looks as if conservatives and liberals were in battle again and there is nothing to connect them. But is this true?

If there is a battle, it is rather political; it cannot be related to a different attitude towards nature. The difference between conservatives and liberals is that the latter want to pay a huge price for our transition to "green energy" and a ban on fossil fuels. It is a matter of money, finances, rather than a different attitude towards nature. The Republican Party makes it clear that someone has to pay the bill and that the American people are not ready for that, especially in the current crisis that began in 2020.

And because most conservatives in America are devout Christians, this is the time to analyze a problem about Christianity and the environment. *Can we combine green movements with Christianity?*

First, we must clarify that *green movements are social and political movements*. They are not based entirely on science and scientific theories. In this sense, their members are susceptible to certain cultural influences. Among them we can mention the interest in Eastern religions (Hinduism, Vedanta, Buddhism, Yoga), as well as the idea of returning to paganism or theosophy. There are many green activists who like yoga, meditation, and therefore are vegetarians or vegans precisely because of such teachings (veganism is very popular in India). This affiliation expresses their need to connect with God and follow the path of spirituality. But they have taken the wrong way to God.

Still, we cannot deny that some green activists are religious. Some of them are Christians, and this should by no means seem absurd. Christians can join and even start green movements. Neither the Church (here we mean the Catholic, but we can talk about other churches), nor the Bible, nor the Doctrine forbid such membership! The only thing they should be careful about is not to succumb to the temptations of paganism or Eastern religions and practices.

As mentioned, green movements have specific cultural aspects. In America, many Greens are interested in yoga and meditation. We can say that this is part of the wave called The New Age. The latter is a specific worldview or approach to reality that emphasizes the mixing of different religions and religious practices. The New Age combines ideas taken from Christianity, Theosophy, Hinduism, Buddhism, yoga, and even Islam. What we see today among the green movements is such a combination of different ideas. Still, the green activists themselves claim that they are not believers. It is true that they believe in some God, but this is not the God of Christians, this is not the God Who inspired the Bible. That is why we can say that these are atheists.

It is important to note that Christianity does not prohibit anyone from joining such movements unless they are overtly anti-Christian. For example, members of a radical communist group cannot be Christians because radical communism is based on the doctrine of "militant atheism." But in the case of green movements, we are not dealing with such radicals. In general, green groups rarely attack Christians and the Church. They believe that their main enemy is "corporations."

In an article published in 2007, the researcher Gregory Hitzhusen analyzes the relationship between Christianity and green movements. He claims that the Christian point of view regarding nature and environment needs to be taught in schools and colleges, and that it does not exclude proper treatment of the environment.

Hitzhusen believes that one of the culprits for the negative attitude towards Christianity in environmental circles is the researcher Lynn White. The latter criticizes Christianity as incompatible with ecology. As Hitzhusen reports, "Examining the roots of the modern ecological crisis, Lynn White argued that Christianity's anthropocentric Western form ... sanctioned and gave rise to a destructive marriage of science and technology" (Hitzhusen 57). This is the theory that Western Christianity (Catholicism and Protestantism) is essentially against nature and approves of the complete control that man has over nature and the world.

However, this is not true, as we will show later. Eastern Christianity (Orthodoxy), for example, is cited by White as an exception. All this means that the problem is not (entirely) due to religion, and there are other factors here. For example, it is a fact that secularism appeared in Western Europe (and the Western world in general) in the 18th century; and then the Orthodox countries were either occupied by Muslims (for example, Greece) or not strong enough politically (Russia). The opposite of the above thesis can even be argued*: it is not Christianity but secularism that is to blame for the uncontrolled destruction of nature by man.*

But there are researchers who prove that the so-called White's thesis is wrong. As Hitzhusen points out, some renowned scholars "detail other cultural factors whose influence on modern environmental attitudes… overshadows the role of Judeo-Christian dogma. These include democratization, materialism, secularization, individualism, and the proliferation of individual wealth" (Hitzhusen 57). The truth is that *environmental problems stem from the idea that man is the master of the world.* But this is not a religious principle and it has nothing to do with Christianity! The Bible, as we will prove, states that man is not a master. Only God can be called that, and man is a humble creation of God.

Other research done outside the United States shows that White's thesis is inaccurate. Christianity has no direct connection to a potential lack of interest in environmental issues. As Hitzhusen observes, "Outside the USA, several cross-national studies explicitly rejected the White Thesis, finding no consistent pattern of difference between Judeo-Christian and non-Judeo-Christian respondents' environmental concern and behavior" (Hitzhusen 59).

On top of all that, it is crucial to emphasize the fact that Christianity has a huge role to play in American society. Although the United States is a secular state, religion is still culturally dominant. We, consciously or not, carry with us the values inherited from our ancestors. As this researcher claims, "In the USA the most common sources of environmental values are spiritual and religious" (Hitzhusen 60). To this we can add the fact that there is no evidence that Christians in the United States mistreat nature or are careless about the environment. Hitzhusen remarks that current sociological projects "do not indicate that conservative Christians demonstrate worse environmental behavior than others do, and recent polls find evangelical Christian views comparable to those of the American public in desiring stronger action to protect the environment" (Hitzhusen 61).

Perhaps the explanation for all this is the lack of trust of Christians in Green NGOs as well as green political groups in general. Christians treat the environment properly, but they do not have sympathy for the political agenda of the Greens. This is because the Greens very often support socialist or liberal views, which irritates most conservatives. And the truth is that environmental protection should not become a means of political influence. At the moment it is a political issue!

As we will see later, ecology is even compatible with theology, and a movement called ecotheology does exist. Ecotheology can be easily studied in all educational institutions without violating the secular principle of separation of state and Church. Gregory Hitzhusen asserts that "ecotheology can contribute to environmental education in public, private, and religious educational contexts, and through informal free-choice learning venues, with each setting offering unique opportunities for incorporation" (Hitzhusen 63). All this means that Christianity and its worldview are unfairly neglected in the field of ecology.

Ecotheology is a branch of theology that emerged in the 1980s in connection with the increased environmental awareness of the people at the time. This subject focuses entirely on the relationship between God, man and nature. Unlike ontology or metaphysics, for example, ecology solves specific problems and gives specific advice on what to do to keep the environment clean. Ontology deals with Being itself; metaphysics deals with the First Principles. But the task of ecology is to understand what the relationship between man and the environment should be in the context of the fact that both are God's creations.

Hitzhusen reports that "Laurel Kearns identifies the three primary traditions of Christian ecotheology in the USA as stewardship, eco-justice, and creation spirituality, and describes representative examples of each type" (Hitzhusen 64). Man was created to serve; by keeping nature clean, man shows his reverence for God, our Creator. As the researcher defines this branch, "'Ecotheology' is used as a general term to refer to theologies or religious teachings that address environmental concerns."

But he believes that this definition is not good for two reasons: "Not all spiritual and religious insights that bear on the environment are considered theology, and theological insights have varying degrees of environmental applicability" (Hitzhusen 67, note 1). The problem with theology is that it focuses on purely philosophical aspects, i.e. the universal dimensions of nature. It does not try to see everything in specific situations. Therefore, it is not very clear whether eco theology is really theology. But even if it is not, this fact does not change anything - the very fact that it exists shows that Christians are concerned about environmental issues.

Ecotheology is an interesting approach to environmental problems, but it does not in itself provide ready-made solutions. The important thing is that it educates Christians to protect nature and be careful with natural resources. As Hitzhusen states, "Ecotheology is no panacea, but various studies show that in the USA ... religious affiliations tend to promote positive environmental behaviors and attitudes rather than discourage them" (Hitzhusen 66).

The subject of this author is specifically the problem of the neglect of academic circles to the Christian worldview, as we will show, this neglect is wrong and leads to additional problems because it reinforces the division between conservatives and liberals. According to him, one of the reasons for this ignorance is the secular nature of the state: "Major factor in the exclusion of Christian and Jewish ethics and theology from environmental education is the secularization of public education in the USA over the past 125 years" (Hitzhusen 56). But his conclusion is that "The notable rise of Jewish and Christian environmental literatures, organizations, and doctrines over the past 35 years also weighs against the suggestion that Biblical beliefs are antithetical to environmental progress" (Hitzhusen 57). Here we see an optimistic prediction that the Christian approach will be accepted and widespread in the near future.

Every in-depth analysis of the Bible and of theology shows that the relation of Christianity to nature is a relation of equal created beings - on one side we find man, and on the other nature. They are comparable in the sense that they are equally a creation of God. It is true that man was created with the highest purpose, but this does not mean that nature is something insignificant.

The researcher Ernst Conradie focuses more on the Church. What is its attitude to environmental issues? According to him, it does not ignore them, but even advises the believers to actively protect nature. Nonetheless, there are some peculiarities here. Let's see what they are.

Conradie exposes his thesis by stating that "The church is not there for its own sake, but for the sake of the salvation of the world. The church will pass away and will become redundant in the eschaton. Christian mission is not merely to expand the church but to transform the world" (Conradie 165). This makes it clear that the Church pursues the salvation of all mankind; but this salvation is not material and is not realized by material means, in a material way. The world is seen as a combination of the spiritual and the material, and in this sense salvation embraces both the bodily and the spiritual essence of man. But *preserving the environment cannot be considered the main goal of the Church, and this must be clear*. The church looks far beyond the material, and environmental problems are precisely related to the material.

If we want to solve environmental problems, we must first look inside ourselves. This environmental crisis is the result of something wrong that we are doing. We need to judge what we are doing wrong and what we need to change.

The real problem is that we have forgotten about God and are only looking after our own interests. Selfishness has overwhelmed us. There is a lack of love and compassion for other living beings. We live in a culture of death, where destruction is taken for granted; a culture in which life and living are not valued. From this point of view, it is quite normal for man's destructive tendencies to dominate.

We must always start from the position that the environment is a creation of God, and it is not right to think that we are masters of nature. As Conradie notes, "What environs the church is God's world. What environs God's world is the triune God. That is the true theological orientation required for the church in addressing environmental threats" (Conradie 168). We will see that a similar text was published by Pope Francis.

The first task of Christians is to save their souls, to be cleansed from sin. But that doesn't mean we have to completely forget about the environment. It is the world we live in. It is part of us, and we are part of it. God created *this* nature, *this* environment, and we should not leave it to ourselves. And we need to realize this. The problem is that we are too slow. As the author states, "In many contexts Christians are not environmental activists and environmental activists are not Christian. The frustration is that churches are slow to respond and are actually contributing to the problem" (Conradie 158).

This is true- Christian communities react more slowly because they have a different goal. However, there are many organizations and groups that deal with environmental issues. They have specialists who work on specific issues. Priests are neither scientists nor experts in the field of ecology.

Some Christians may wonder why we need to protect the environment. Do these problems affect us? As Conradie asks, "If Jesus is coming again soon, and if the world is going to be destroyed in any case, why would there be any need to care for the earth now?" (Conradie 158).

But *all this comes from a misunderstanding of the doctrine of salvation*. Christ never said that we should completely ignore this world. Salvation is not achieved by denying the world (including the environment), but by denying the carnal, the sinful, the sin. Love of God means to love his creation as well; for, God created this creation and saw that it was good. If it was not good, God would not have created it!

We cannot stand passively and just look at the injustice and evil that exists. We must fight them. At the same time, we must be able to reconcile; to accept evil as such, because thanks to it we know what is good, what is light, what is love. God is not to blame for the presence of ecological issues and disasters. But the world cannot be perfect, at least because of Original Sin.

But the Christian community is not absolutely in harmony regarding the environment. There are different points of view within Christianity itself. This is noted by Conradie as follows: "Theologically speaking, the stages of negotiation and acceptance represent the whole current debate in the field of Christian ecotheology, in all its complexity and distinct discourses" (Conradie 159). Different churches and denominations have their own points of view. Therefore, one cannot speak of a unified position of all Christian churches.

One example is the idea of serving as guardians of nature. Should we be like that? Is this our ontological status? As this researcher writes, "calls for environmental stewardship are also heavily criticized in ecumenical circles. At the heart of this critique are questions about the hierarchical position assigned to human beings within the earth community." Conradie explains that "If humans are to be stewards, God is either portrayed as being at the top of the hierarchy or as an absentee landlord. As many others have observed, this is hardly the model required amidst critiques of anthropocentrism" (Conradie 160).

The relationship between God and man is at the heart of Christian theology. Man must listen to God and keep His Commandments. On the other hand, one must take care of the environment in which one lives. Of course, there are different interpretations of the latter statement. According to some theologians, we do not need to care much about the environment, as long as our salvation has nothing to do with it. Whether we solve environmental crises or not, we must seek our salvation. Even if we stop climate change, it will not change our chances of survival. Our salvation depends mainly on the Will of God, or more precisely, on His Grace.

Ernst Conradie's conclusion is this: *The church must advise believers to care for the environment, without this being their most important goal*. As he writes, "There is, of course, little need for Christian churches to duplicate the work of other environmental organizations. Churches should, instead, support the work of these organizations as far as possible" (Conradie 161). In short, believers need to be informed that there are such and such environmental problems and that there are such and such organizations that claim to be able to deal with them.

This position is slightly skeptical, as it is based on the idea that Christians should not think about the environment first. The author is right in saying that salvation is our first goal. However, we must also express our love for the world, insofar as we are equal to it in our status as creatures.

Now is the time to turn to the question of how the Bible and Christianity can change our view of the environment and its problems in general.

4.2 The Christian view on the environment

Summary:

Here we will refer to some passages from the Bible to show that God's Will is that man should have respect and love for nature. Man and nature are coequal, although man stands higher in an ontological sense. We will also refer to *Laudato si*, an Encyclical letter by Pope Francis, which describes the Church's view on environmental problems.

Christian views on the environment are difficult to bring together into a single theory, as one has not yet been formulated. Ecotheology sets itself such a task, but there is no harmony and unity of views in it. Some of its representatives are not professional theologians.

Here we will turn to two different sources of Christian views on nature, and we will prove our thesis with quotations from the Holy Scriptures.

Our thesis is as follows: *man must take care of the environment. In this way he shows his love and respect for our Creator*. One of the basic principles of Christianity is love and compassion for other people. But it is important to clarify that even if one does not take care of nature, man does not commit sin. Ignoring environmental issues alone is not a sin. But sin is at the root of the wrong attitude towards nature. This means that we must eliminate the specific sin that is the cause of this attitude.

We will first refer to Jeremaia Waqainabete, a Methodist pastor from Fiji. This is a small island nation that would be in serious danger of melting glaciers. His position supports environmental activism. According to this pastor, global warming is evident and countries like Fiji are at high risk. But not only the people of Fiji, but all Christians need to think about what they can do about it. As Waqainabete states, "The present dilemma of climate change and global warming that is threatening the terrestrial existence highlights the shattered state of the Sabbath, rest and the Shalom of God as human beings become self-centered as we are driven by the spirit of greed" (Waqainabete 9).

As we have already explained, man has begun to consider himself the center of the world, from which our environmental problems arise. We have already seen that destructive human activities, including deforestation and environmental pollution, are not encouraged by Christianity. We cannot find their justification in Christian theology.

The author seeks the cause of our troubles in Original Sin, which led to the appearance of evil in the world. Undoubtedly, the blame for this lies with man. We cannot blame God just because we have environmental problems today. Waqainabete observes that "Man's missing the divine intent (sin) disrupted God's universal order and man lost his status and the earth was cursed and likewise all its inhabitants became distorted" (Waqainabete 9). The presence of evil is something that is associated with environmental crises; because these crises are evil! As we noted, this does not mean that this world is evil or that we do evil by nature. The world is good insofar as it is God's creation; and we have the opportunity to increase the goodness in it by helping, loving, and feeling compassion.

The preacher from Fiji goes on to say, "We are encouraged to realize that our whole existence is to be worthy of God therefore all things done in life should be seen in the light of it being done in the presence of God" (Waqainabete 14). We must always look to God, to his Word, to his advice. We should not neglect God when we talk about the environment, because it is exactly part of his creation.

Waqainabete remarks that "We are called to deal with the environment and creation in the manner that is right and proper with God" (Waqainabete 14). This means that we should not deny the role of God in this process; for example, some green organizations are based on atheistic ideology and even believe that religion hinders the solution of environmental problems. But this understanding is wrong - it is precisely the result of the misconception that man is the highest rational being and that he can completely control nature.

But the Bible says that we are equal to other beings, even though we possess intellect. This is what should make us respect other living beings, as the preacher notes: "It is a must that we acknowledge the dignity of all living things and treat them in a manner that is worthy of God the Creator, and in due course uphold our stewardship roles as designated and instituted by God" (Waqainabete 21). This is further confirmed by Pope Francis with a document which will be discussed later.

Waqainabete believes that we have a role to play as conservationists. Of course, this opinion is personal and can be criticized. For example, we may ask: is it not God's job to protect living beings and the world He has created in general? How do we know that we are the guardians of nature? In what follows, we will refer to several passages from the Bible that show exactly that. And yet, nowhere is it written that man must solve all the crises, all the problems of this world.

According to Waqainabete, we are part of a whole chain and we cannot escape our responsibility to the world. We are the image and likeness of God, and therefore we have a specific role: "Our interdependence is understood in the ecosystem chain and the role of human beings in this chain is far much greater because the image of God in man is personified in the physical and spiritual components that make us human beings" (Waqainabete 7).

God is the master and Creator of this world, and we are his image. It follows that we have the right to interfere in various natural phenomena, as long as we do not contradict God's commandments and instructions. As the Fijian preacher writes, "Our ability to take care of the universe and all creation can only be displayed to its totality when we are in the image of God and the image of God can only surface in our lives when we are completely open and obedient to God" (Waqainabete 8). It follows that we must be loyal to God and keep His commandments. But the question remains: is there any of His commandments that refers specifically to the environment?

Of course, environmental issues are relatively novel, and we cannot expect to find an answer to this question in the Bible. However, there are passages that relate in some way to environmental issues. Waqainabete's conclusion is logical: "We do not exist in isolation from the rest of the world as we share life with other living things in God's universe where we are destined to experience and enjoy the fullness of life according to the Divine intent" (Waqainabete 25).

This position encourages environmental activism, linking this activism to the principles of mutual aid, compassion, and altruism. Undoubtedly, an optimistic understanding of the world can be seen here, whereas Original Sin still leaves its traces on this world. It is always good to keep this in mind and not forget that our first goal must be *salvation*.

There is no doubt that Waqainabete's publication aims to encourage Christians in a particular region - the Pacific state of Fiji - to become more active and help reduce environmental problems. Although he places too much emphasis on "global warming", other threats are also real - air and ocean pollution, the excessive use of plastic, the need to recycle waste. The solution to these problems begins with the individual. If we do not do something ourselves, there will be no one else to do it. We must be active and not leave everything to others. As Waqainabete writes, "All these acts for the better begin with individuals and that is you and I. So as we speak of being practical Christians and responsible people we are speaking of individuals (you and I) to kick start this lifestyle by doing what you have to do for the betterment of all" (Waqainabete 24).

Now is the time to move on to what we can find in the Bible about environmental issues. Is it true that we should not think about the world around us, but should think only and constantly about our salvation? This is not entirely true.

We can find various topics and problems in Holy Scripture. Generally speaking, environmental issues are addressed in the context of the relationship between God and man. Man is a part of the world, of creation, and as such he must understand his limitations.

In the Book of *Genesis*, we find the story of the Creation and the initial moments of the existence of mankind. In Chapter 1, we read how God created all animals and he said that all that was good. Then, human beings were created:

> Then God said, "Let us make man in
> our image, in our likeness, and let them
> rule over the fish of the sea and the
> birds of the air, over the livestock, over

all the earth, and over all the creatures
that move along the ground." (Gen. 1:25-26; *New International Version*)

This passage is ambiguous. It can be interpreted differently. According to some people, it means that we have the right to control the life of all living beings, including nature. But is this true?

We must not forget that God has only given us permission to dominate, to rule. This does not mean that everything is allowed to us! In *Psalms*, we find a crucial passage regarding the role of God as Our Creator:

He makes springs pour water into the
ravines; it flows between the mountains.
They give water to all the beasts of the
field; the wild donkeys quench their
thirst.
The birds of the air nest by the waters;
they sing among the branches.
He waters the mountains from his
upper chambers; the earth is satisfied
by the fruit of his work.
He makes grass grow for the cattle,
and plants for man to cultivate- bringing
forth food from the earth. (Ps. 104:10-14)

Here we see how life exists and flows thanks to Him. Animals have food and water thanks to God; everything exists through Him and thanks to Him! But man is not God; man is not the Creator. Therefore, man cannot take life or destroy what God has created. This is one of the basic principles of Christianity, and we can say that it is a principle of the culture of life.

If we accept the opposite thesis, namely that man is a completely independent entity and he can dominate the whole world, then we would come to the conclusion that he can easily destroy and build according to his will. But when another Will stands above the human, then this right is limited. Man did not create the world; he did not create the mountains, the oceans, the animals. From this point of view, the fate of all of these is not in his hands.

In the Book of *Job* we find another passage describing the proper relation between man and nature. In this book, Job is concerned with showing his righteousness and arguing with his friends to prove that the Wisdom of God is above their reason. He states the following to his friends:

> "But ask the animals, and they will
> teach you, or the birds of the air, and
> they will tell you;
> or speak to the earth, and it will teach
> you, or let the fish of the sea inform you.
> Which of all these does not know that

> the hand of the Lord has done this?
> In his hand is the life of every creature
> and the breath of all mankind. (Job 12:7-10)

These words can be interpreted as leading to complete passivity. But we said that the issue of environmental activity could be interpreted differently. Some churches and priests believe that we need to be more active in the field of environmental protection; but this does not mean that this is a unified and official position of the Church.

The passages we quote here demonstrate that God has all the knowledge and Wisdom to know what to do with the world. But He also guides, instructs us what to do with nature. In these passages we can find some indications that we must respect the order in nature and should not destroy it. In practice, man is guilty of violating this order not only with Original Sin, but also with the very idea that man is the center of the world.

In our opinion, it is not right to interpret all this in the direction of passivity. As we have already shown, nature is part of the created world, and so we are compared to animals, plants, planets, and everything else.

Specific nature conservation tips can also be found in some passages. Although thousands of years ago such a problem did not really exist (there was no industrialization, nor were the forests cut down), a passage suggests that one advice can still be found on ecology. This passage can be found in the Book of *Numbers* and reads as follows:

> "Do not pollute the land where you
> are. Bloodshed pollutes the land, and

> atonement cannot be made for the land
> on which blood has been shed, except
> by the blood of the one who shed it.
> Do not defile the land where you live
> and where I dwell, for I, the Lord , dwell
> among the Israelites." (Num. 35:33-34)

We must keep our land clean because it was given to us by the Lord. Of course, this passage can be interpreted more as a prohibition on making sacrifices (as far as they come from paganism), but we can still find the idea of purity. The Lord Himself is among the Israelites, therefore He is among us at all times; and we must know that we must maintain cleanliness and order.

In the description of the end of the world that we can see in the Bible, we find another interesting fact. Christian eschatology is, in fact, a vivid picture of a crumbling world, a world steeped in destruction and suffering. But in this description, we also see natural disasters. In the Book of *Revelation* the reader can find some significant details:

> The second angel sounded his trumpet,
> and something like a huge mountain, all
> ablaze, was thrown into the sea. A third
> of the sea turned into blood,
> a third of the living creatures in the sea
> died, and a third of the ships were

> destroyed.
>
> The third angel sounded his trumpet,
> and a great star, blazing like a torch, fell
> from the sky on a third of the rivers and
> on the springs of water-
> the name of the star is Wormwood. A
> third of the waters turned bitter, and
> many people died from the waters that
> had become bitter.
>
> The fourth angel sounded his trumpet,
> and a third of the sun was struck, a third
> of the moon, and a third of the stars, so
> that a third of them turned dark. A third
> of the day was without light, and also a
> third of the night. (Rev. 8:7-12)

In this description we see well a picture of dead animals, natural disasters, destruction. The overall context of the book shows that the end of the world is associated with unusual phenomena, broken laws, the destruction of the false harmony that exists in the world. It is no coincidence that in some natural disasters (for example, Chernobyl, which we have already analyzed), people recall this passage and claim that it is a prophecy that applies specifically to Chernobyl.

Eschatology has something to do with green activists, and more specifically with radical ones. We call them alarmists, but in fact they can also be called "false prophets." What they do is based on a particular interpretation of the Book of *Revelation*. The picture they paint is a false prophecy; it is false because it has nothing to do with God, and only God really knows what the future holds. God's Wisdom is infinite, and we cannot speak on His behalf. Yes, alarmists do not believe in God, and that is a fact; but they are trying to play the role of the ancient prophets of Israel!

One reader may note that in the book of *Revelation* we see only symbols. And this is completely true; but there are many symbols in the Bible, which does not mean that the prophecies in it have a purely symbolic value. The struggle between the Lamb of God and the enemy of the human race, for example, is not symbolic at all; the hellfire described in the same book is quite real. That is why we can believe that a colossal environmental disaster will occur as a sign of the Second Coming of Christ.

But this does not mean that this disaster is the very end of the world. These are two different events that have no causal link. The hail, the reddening of the water, the extinction of the animals, the appearance of the comet are *signs* that show that the end of this world is coming, and with it a new beginning will come.

Without a doubt, the task we set ourselves must be our salvation. But if we continue to destroy nature, cut down forests, pollute the air, water and soil, we risk causing many problems to the human race. Not that humanity will disappear; but in this way we amplify the destructive impulse within us, that impulse which actually makes us walk the path of sin.

In any case, the main task of the Church is to deal with the eternal and the unchangeable; we must strive for God, for our Creator. Nature, the environment are transient beings; they are not something absolute. So even radical green activists are wrong: not everything depends on us. *The will and wisdom of God must guide us properly*. We must pray that He will find the right solution before us. Also, our prayers can make the world a better place; they can reduce natural disasters, help us protect the environment.

But all this depends on the Will of God. As Pope Francis observes in his Encyclical letter *Laudato si* (2015), "A spirituality which forgets God as all-powerful and Creator is not acceptable. That is how we end up worshipping earthly powers, or ourselves usurping the place of God, even to the point of claiming an unlimited right to trample his creation underfoot" (Laudato si sect. 75). We need to look to Him again, because without God we are powerless and cannot think of any right solution.

The fact is that over time, humanity has coped better with natural disasters. Today we have equipment with which we can predict earthquakes, intense storms, tsunamis, and other dangerous phenomena. We have the opportunity to quickly warn citizens about the need to defend themselves. All this happens with God's help and His approval. Modern technologies are not only a threat but also an opportunity; thanks to them we can protect human life better than humans could 2-3 centuries ago. But these technologies sometimes make us overconfident, overly proud. We believe in "progress" and that it is infinite; in that all people will live better in time.

However, Pope Paul VI criticizes this attitude in his Apostolic letter *Octogesima adveniens* (1971). As he puts it, "What is the meaning of this never-ending, breathless pursuit of a progress that always eludes one just when one believes one has conquered it sufficiently in order to enjoy it in peace? If it is not attained, it leaves one dissatisfied" (Octogesima sect. 41). Although we have these modern technologies, we still remain fragile and extreme beings.

Octogesima adveniens is an apostolic letter devoted to a large number of contemporary problems. The letter focuses mainly on social issues, such as poverty and inequality; but it also shows what the roots of socialism are and how it can be repudiated from the point of view of Christianity. In the letter, we find the first definition of environmental crisis written by the Head of the Catholic Church. Although there are only three paragraphs devoted to environmental issues, the following quote is very interesting: "Not only is the material environment becoming a permanent menace - pollution and refuse, new illness and absolute destructive capacity- but the human framework is no longer under man's control" (Octogesima sect. 21). The cause of environmental problems is clearly stated - man no longer has the strength to stop the processes that began in the age of modernity. Such processes are rapid industrialization, urbanization, mass emigration. Nature also suffers because of them.

This Apostolic letter was not focused clearly on environmental issues. This is why something new was needed. Another document was issued to address the environmental crisis we face today.

Pope Francis goes in the same direction like Pope Paul VI. He wrote an Encyclical letter to address environmental issues properly. In his Letter, all significant issues are shown clearly: what are the reasons for the current ecological crisis; what are the particular issues; what can we do. Pope Francis offers dialogue and mutual understanding in the name of our common well-being. He refers to Christian values and demonstrates that we need to turn to God again and to pay homage to Him; we need to love and take care of all living beings and of "our sister" - the earth.

As Pope Francis begins his Letter, "This sister now cries out to us because of the harm we have inflicted on her by our irresponsible use and abuse of the goods with which God has endowed her." As he goes on, "The violence present in our hearts, wounded by sin, is also reflected in the symptoms of sickness evident in the soil, in the water, in the air and in all forms of life" (Laudato si sect. 2). Pope Francis also speaks of the fact that this crisis stems from our tendency to make mistakes, from our conviction that man controls everything. But we cannot find such a statement in the Bible - man is not the center of the universe, and this is more than obvious. As Francis writes, "Although it is true that we Christians have at times incorrectly interpreted the Scriptures, nowadays we must forcefully reject the notion that our being created in God's image and given dominion over the earth justifies absolute domination over other creatures" (Laudato si sect 67). The pope opposes the claim that Christianity is to blame for this.

Pope Francis takes inspiration from the renowned medieval saint St. Francis of Assisi. He was a remarkable man who interacted with animals and plants. He believed in the good and in the power of compassion. His actions were based on the idea that all living beings are interconnected because they are creations of God. The Pope states that "Saint Francis is the example par excellence of care for the vulnerable and of an integral ecology lived out joyfully and authentically. He is the patron saint of all who study and work in the field of ecology, and he is also much loved by non-Christians" (Laudato si sect. 10).

Integral ecology is an interesting concept that we see in this document. This concept covers various areas, such as ecology, social sphere, culture, economy. We cannot solve environmental problems without looking at poverty and inequality today. We know that this pope pays special attention to social issues, and to a certain extent he has a socialist bias. Therefore, it does not seem strange that he wants to emphasize the role of poverty in the emergence of environmental crises.

According to Pope Francis, we must realize that our freedom is not limitless. Its limits are set within reason and morality. At the same time, we must be careful with selfish interests and desires that can drive us to outrageous and immoral things. Pope Francis asserts that "human beings are not completely autonomous. Our freedom fades when it is handed over to the blind forces of the unconscious, of immediate needs, of self-interest, and of violence ... we stand naked and exposed in the face of our ever-increasing power" (Laudato si sect 105). As we have already shown, new technologies not only give power, but are also obstacles to our spiritual life. We must not obey machines, new technologies (which exist not only in the field of machines, but also in many other fields, such as biology); we must carefully control our desires, especially if they are destructive.

Pope Francis declares that our culture is wrong; this means that our attitude and attitude towards the world in general are wrong. As he argues, environmental issues "are closely linked to a throwaway culture which affects the excluded just as it quickly reduces things to rubbish. To cite one example, most of the paper we produce is thrown away and not recycled" (Laudato si sect. 22). On the one hand, we have a society that throws away a lot of things (not just garbage, but also stuff that can be used or consumed by other people). It consumes a lot of resources and does not even realize that these resources can be depleted. On the other side is the other half of humanity, living in poverty and inequality. It cannot use most of these resources, and the saddest thing is that for several dollars monthly pay it produces products that then end up in the trash.

Here, Pope Francis is right to change our attitude towards goods and try to use them for as long as possible. This is again the idea of a circular economy; and yet, as we have shown, a circular economy in the complete sense of the word is impossible because it will reduce jobs and lead to another type of poverty.

Pope Francis calls for a change in our way of life (as long as we are part of the "happy half" of mankind), in order to reduce environmental issues: "Humanity is called to recognize the need for changes of lifestyle, production and consumption, in order to combat this warming or at least the human causes which produce or aggravate it" (Laudato si sect. 23). Here the pope focuses on the alleged global warming, which according to this document is a result of human activity: "It is true that there are other factors (such as volcanic activity, variations in the earth's orbit and axis, the solar cycle), yet a number of scientific studies indicate that most global warming in recent decades is due to the great concentration of greenhouse gases" (Laudato si sect. 23).

Here Pope Francis refers to scientific research; he does not want to get into discussions about whether all this is true. According to this document, the Church must have trust in scientists, and it can only support the search for solutions: "On many concrete questions, the Church has no reason to offer a definite opinion; she knows that honest debate must be encouraged among experts, while respecting divergent views" (Laudato si sect. 61). But there are also obvious environmental problems, such as pollution and drinking water problems; about them, there is no need to look for scientific data, Pope Francis writes, because we all see them. Elsewhere, he notes that "the Church does not presume to settle scientific questions or to replace politics. But I am concerned to encourage an honest and open debate so that particular interests or ideologies will not prejudice the common good" (Laudato si sect. 188).

Any dialogue between politicians, citizens, economists, and other stakeholders should not be avoided. The bad thing is that people are often driven by selfish interests instead of community interests. According to Pope Francis, "many efforts to seek concrete solutions to the environmental crisis have proved ineffective, not only because of powerful opposition but also because of a more general lack of interest" (Laudato si sect. 14). One half of humanity lives peacefully and away from environmental problems, while the other half has neither the power nor the resources to solve them. Here, Pope Francis is right - there is a proven link between poverty and environmental problems, because it is not only large factories that pollute; so do poor households that rely on wood, coal, and some households in India even burn garbage. That is why the cities in India are the most polluted in the world.

Rapid urbanization and population growth in a limited number of major cities around the world create opportunities for environmental crises. As stated in this document, "We are aware of the disproportionate and unruly growth of many cities, which have become unhealthy to live in, not only because of pollution caused by toxic emissions but also as a result of urban chaos, poor transportation, and visual pollution and noise." This growth is too fast and therefore resource problems arise: "Many cities are huge, inefficient structures, excessively wasteful of energy and water" (Laudato si sect. 44).

All this does not mean that we should think about reducing the population of our planet; the problem is the unequal distribution of the population and the fact that big cities (especially in the Third World) do not have good conditions for newcomers. Good living and working conditions must be provided in small settlements so that people do not have to emigrate to large cities or other countries. But these problems, according to Pope Francis, must be solved by the international community. He does not write it explicitly, but he means that the rich countries must take their share and help the poor (which is actually happening).

Pope Francis draws attention to the fact that the Christian community must serve as our example for dealing with environmental problems. We must be united and in solidarity, and we must show love and compassion for the world around us: "Care for nature is part of a lifestyle which includes the capacity for living together and communion" (Laudato si sect. 228). Society and nature are connected, they cannot be considered separate entities. As we read in this Letter, "When we speak of the 'environment', what we really mean is a relationship existing between nature and the society which lives in it ... We are part of nature, included in it and thus in constant interaction with it" (Laudato si sect. 139). Man is not entirely isolated from nature; and the Church believes that respect for nature is part of our moral obligations.

This principle seems obvious to many Christians, but there are still believers who are not interested in this issue. It is therefore reasonable to pay more attention to our attitude towards nature, especially in the context of these environmental problems. It does not matter who of us is a believer and who is not; we have a common goal when it comes to nature- to protect it. The Letter states that "Whether believers or not, we are agreed today that the earth is essentially a shared inheritance, whose fruits are meant to benefit everyone. For believers, this becomes a question of fidelity to the Creator, since God created the world for everyone" (Laudato si sect. 93). The earth is our common home, and this is not only a metaphor, it is the reality.

The love for life, for living beings, and for nature in general has its concrete dimensions. We have a duty to love one another as we love God and as we love ourselves. But our selfish interests make us do things that are not moral. Pope Francis gives one such example - abortion. It is an expression of disrespect for life. As he notes, "concern for the protection of nature is also incompatible with the justification of abortion. How can we genuinely teach the importance of concern for other vulnerable beings ... if we fail to protect a human embryo" (Laudato si sect. 120).

In connection with the latter, we can say that it is strange that green movements protect, for example, animal rights and encourage us to eat less meat (which, according to them, also causes global warming); but, on the other hand, these movements not only do not oppose abortion, but even support it! This is hypocritical, and it seems that the primary purpose of such movements is not to protect nature; or at least, they do not see the whole picture because their horizon is too narrow and small.

The Encyclical letter *Laudato si* (2015) gives us food for thought. It shows that we need to see all crises as interconnected - because economic crises lead to poverty, and poverty leads to diseases and environmental problems.

The Letter also talks about integrated ecology. This means that we solve environmental problems together with economic and social ones. There is no way to solve them separately.

The shortcomings of this Letter is that it offers only a discussion. An agreement must be sought within the Catholic Church on all the issues described in the Letter. The Church needs to be more active not only in social but also in environmental and economic issues. Today we live in another economic crisis that will leave many people without a home or a job; the Church needs to take care of these people and attract them. Only the Church can offer the right solution in the time of spiritual crisis, when people live under stress, when they have lost their goal in life. Environmental problems need to be addressed with reference to their causes, to their roots. They have not appeared out of nothing; man causes most of them such as deforestation, decreasing energy resources, pollution.

But the root of these issues is not the Church or the Christian worldview. We can find the root of all ecological problems in our ambition to control the world, to dominate over everything. *We have forgotten about God, about the fact that He is omniscient and all-powerful*. Who are we to decide what the future of this planet should be? All our discussions and solutions have to take into account the Christian conception of the Lord.

4.3 Eco-Humanism as a false alternative to Christianity

Summary:

Here we turn to a possible amalgam of Christianity and anthropocentrism. Henryk Skolimowski believes that we need to be united in the face of all contemporary issues, including ecology. However, his point of view omits God and this is his serious mistake.

Any solution to the environmental crisis should start from God and the relation between God and man.

We should look carefully at all doctrines that contain the word "humanism" in their name, or are based on humanism. Humanism is a philosophical doctrine, or attitude, according to which man is the center of the world. It puts stress on human dignity, freedom and autonomy of will. However, it usually rejects the existence of God. Here we will turn to one interesting teaching which tries to combine Christianity with humanism.

The Polish and American philosopher Henryk Skolimowski is one of the most renowned intellectuals that deal with eco philosophy, eco theology, and other philosophical and religious teachings that are centered on ecology. He is among the founders of eco theology; however, his views are not completely orthodox, i.e. he does not found his ideas on the Church doctrine.

From Eco-theology, Skolimowski moved to Eco-philosophy and even Eco-Yoga. It is not clear what are the reasons for this transition; however, we will refer to one of his publications to discuss the problem of the relation between God, man and nature. In his opinion, mankind needs religion but in the context of evolution. As he remarks, "Culture and religion are an inherent part of the human strategies for survival and well being" (Skolimowski sect. 3). His position on Christianity is ambiguous and it is difficult to say whether he seriously believes in Christian doctrines. Nevertheless, the facts show that he is trying to build a bridge between theology and ecology, which is a severe challenge.

Skolimowski puts emphasis on the need to be united and to solve the problems of mankind together. Starting from Kant's Categorical Imperative (a basic principle of

Kant's ethics), the Polish and American philosopher states that we need a modern ethic to address environmental issues. As he puts it, "What unites us ... is care and concern for the preservation and well-being of the whole planet, with all of its creatures. This is what I call the Ecological Imperative. We all share this imperative. And it should be a uniting force, guiding our action and reflection" (Skolimowski sect. 1). An imperative is a moral principle from which all our actions derive; he guides our behavior.

Skolimowski here addresses the problem of technological progress. Does progress have anything to do with environmental destruction? Can we say that they are absolutely opposite? According to him, the problem with technology is that we have stayed too far from our roots. He refers to the german philosopher Oswald Spengler, who speaks of culture as a tactic for living. As Skolimowski argues, "Modern technology, or better — Western technology, has failed us not because it has become ecologically devastating, but mainly because it has forgotten its basic function, namely that all technics are, in the last resort, the tactics for living" (Skolimowski sect. 3). This means that culture, science and all other areas of human activity are the way we live; life remains the highest value, and technology is no longer interested in that value.

Modern technologies are not in complete contradiction with ecology. As we have seen in this book, "environmentally friendly" technologies, or "green technologies," are already developed. But the problem is in our very attitude to technology as something omnipresent and omnipotent; if we have a problem, technology will solve it. Today we do not rely on ourselves, but on computers; we rely on machines, on the Internet, on the means of communication and information. Skolimowski sympathizes with evolutionary theory, even though he himself is a devout Christian; but let us not forget that he was an emigrant who had fled communist Poland, and militant atheism was common there. More or less, it affected him. The belief that there is evolution was necessary to enable a person to survive physically in such conditions. Thus, it is not surprising that he combines some ideas of the materialist worldview with Christianity.

Speaking of Marxism, Skolimowski clarified that the ecological humanism he proposed was not a Marxist doctrine. According to him, "Ecological Humanism has little to do with traditional humanism; and it quite sharply separates itself from Marxist or Socialist humanism, which calls… for the appropriation of Nature to man" (Skolimowski sect. 3). This teaching, or rather a movement, aims to restore harmony between man and nature by placing man and his activities in the context of evolution (which is both material and spiritual).

What exactly is ecological humanism? It has nothing to do with the humanism of the French existentialists, nor with the humanism of the Renaissance philosophers who deny the Church and religion. As Skolimowski states, "Ecological Humanism signifies, among other things, frugality, recycling, the reverence for Nature, which are really three different aspects of the same thing" (Skolimowski sect. 3).

Isn't there a complete denial of the role of God here? Where is God in such a picture of the world? The reader can safely ask these questions, and he will have every right to do so. Ecological humanism is not ecology; it cannot replace it. Furthermore, it begins with man instead of the Creator of the world. Why should we honor nature as an entity written in capital letters? Only God should be written that way, because otherwise we deny His role in creation. Every true care for nature begins with the insight that we exist through the Lord.

Skolimowski's next words confirm this criticism. It requires all of us to trust ourselves as a community; he speaks of service. As he writes, "Ecological Humanism points towards social relationships based on the idea of sharing, and stewardship, rather than owning things and fighting continuous ruthless battles in open and camouflaged social wars" (Skolimowski sect. 3). But the teaching that sees nature as divine is called pantheism; thus, we find some traces of it here. This cannot be called a thesis and has little to do with Christianity. The following words prove it: "It sees the world not as a place for pillage and plunder, an arena for gladiators, but as a sanctuary in which we temporarily dwell, and of which we must take the utmost care" (Skolimowski sect. 3).

Yes, the world is a sanctuary, but we do not learn much about the Creator of the world from these words and from this article at all. Nature as a sanctuary can mean that nature itself is divine! Ad we need to repudiate such a thesis because it is simply not true.

This is the basis of our critique of Skolimowski. Despite his positive attitude toward the Catholic Church and Christianity in general, his teachings must be criticized.

At the end of the article, we find a definition of the so-called Ecological Person. It is "the creature of evolution. It emerges at a certain juncture of human evolution and will disappear at another juncture, when evolution (through us) will transcend itself further." This person is an embodiment of all important Christian values, but the word "Christian" is not mentioned here. As Skolimowski explains further, "Ecological Person recognizes the redeeming and necessary nature of suffering, of compassion, of love of wisdom" (Skolimowski sect. 4). In short, this Person behaves according to Christian values, and yet it does not recognize the origin of these values- God.

Obviously, this theory of evolution is vague and poorly proven. The ideas of the Polish and American philosopher are related to those of Henri Bergson, and both authors have sympathy for religion and the search for truth. But while Bergson's teaching is more a reaction to the crude materialism of Darwinism in the early 20th century, Skolimowski's doctrine is difficult to explain. If we accept that we will ever transcend ourselves, then there remains serious doubt about the idea of man's extremity, his fragility. Why not assume that man is actually God but he simply does not know it? This is how short the path from ecological humanism to The New Age movement is.

True eco philosophy needs to grasp the world as a creation of a superior Power. It is wrong to claim that the world itself is a Power, or that we should venerate it. *The world in itself cannot be its own creator*! The Prime Mover (according to Aristotle) cannot be what is being moved. The First Cause (according to St. Thomas Aquinas) cannot be the same as what is caused. Further, man cannot be held to be the master of the world, because he simply is not a master. Man is fragile and weak, finite and poor in his capacities and abilities. How could we think of ourselves as the most powerful beings? It was the big illusion of the Renaissance and the age of modernity.

4.4. Conclusion

In this chapter we saw that the attitude of the Church and Christianity towards environmental problems should not be passive. The thesis that Christianity is to blame for this ecological crisis (White's thesis) is not true. In fact, the problem is precisely the secularization and denial of the church doctrine. *Industrialization is not rooted in*

Christianity; it was a process of separating of Church and economic power. The economy became an autonomous entity that could not be controlled anymore. Thus, secularization appeared. What has the Church to do with all this?

However, the proponents of a passive attitude to these problems would say: whatever we do, our ultimate goal is salvation. But, as we have already shown, our salvation cannot be based on the denial of Christian values - and they are love and compassion. There is no theologian who will say that we must be completely passive, and God will intervene and solve all problems. We have already shown, by referring to the Bible, that we must show our respect and reverence for the Creator by loving His creation.

Green movements are not self-sufficient. Every social group, every organization can act in order to solve environmental problems. The Church can do the same, but without neglecting our primary goal — salvation and the restoration of the original relationship between God and man. The green movements are not the main enemy of the Church, although there are atheists among them, as well as adherents of Indian religions and paganism. Christians can be part of such movements, as long as they do not deny Christianity and the Church, nor do they force them to do something immoral.

The Christian worldview provides a great alternative to the green movements, and especially to alarmists. Our liberals need to keep this fact in mind because they tend to accuse Christians of anything bad, anything negative in this country. But Liberals are completely wrong.

It is not true that Christianity makes people unaware of the current environmental crisis. Christianity allows people to calm down, not to be afraid of future cataclysms. We need to make rational decisions, not decisions based on emotions and fear. Religion is not fear; it is respect for our Lord, for our Creator. We love Him and we need to love all other living beings. Our destructive instincts need to be controlled, and the only way to do this is by turning to God.

Conclusion

The green movements are very popular today. Many young people belong or want to belong to them. People think that this is the only way to solve modern environmental problems.

These problems are real. We see with our own eyes the polluted air, water, soil. We see the climate changing; winters used to be heavier, with more snow. There really is less snow now, and besides, summer comes later and winter comes later. In short, the seasons are "moving" forward.

In addition, we produce too much garbage and waste too many resources. For example, we individually use much more water on average per day than people in the Third World use in a week. This is just one example of wasting resources. It is not so difficult to save both water and electricity.

As we can see, there are environmental problems that are caused by man; there are also those for whom the claim that they are caused by man is disputable. The former include deforestation, and the latter include global warming and climate change.

As we have shown, it cannot be said with absolute certainty that the human factor is most important in this case. There are various factors for global warming (if it is real), and it is indisputable that in the past there has been global warming even without human involvement. Furthermore, we cannot look back more than 100 years to see what the carbon data in the atmosphere were. We are just taking measurements recently, so there is no way to be sure what exactly is the rise of these emissions into the atmosphere.

At the same time, however, we are forced to take action as if man alone is responsible for this increase or change. "Green policies" are being implemented, leading to a reduction in the use of fossil fuels and the introduction of "green technologies". There is talk of a global ban on fossil fuels around the middle of this century. Do we have the resources to continue to sustain our economy without relying on fossil fuels or nuclear energy? The Texas crisis is not the only case. This is an example that shows that an unprepared system will have huge problems with its energy capacity. Green policies assume that winters will become milder, and therefore the southern states will not need much energy in winter. But in Texas we saw the opposite!

However, we must clarify that this book is not intended to work with scientific data or to confirm or refute scientific hypotheses and theories. Our goal is to show what the green organizations and activists are, what their main views are, whether they have anything to do with socialism, and whether they offer a real alternative to the current economy. In our opinion, green organizations are political and social movements that do not rely much on real scientific data. They work with certain dogmas and attitudes, on the basis of which they take specific actions and organize campaigns.

Caring for nature and the environment is not limited to the green movements. It also has alternatives. In the present work, we present the Christian views on nature. In fact, *the environmental problems we have are the result of rapid industrialization and the lack of any ethical control in this area*. It is only in the last three or four decades that governments around the world have begun to think about the environment. And the Christian point of view is clear: we must love nature as we love God, because He created us and nature. We must not destroy it, we must not harm it. The idea that man is the center of the world leads to the fact that he destroys forests and builds huge cities in which there is terrible poverty. If we had looked at the Christian worldview earlier, we would have moved very moderately along the path of technological progress, and perhaps these problems would not have arisen.

We must not forget that this progress continues today. New technologies are being created that aim to overcome nature. There is talk of DNA programming, to eliminate predisposition to disease through gene therapy; there is talk of creating a mixed organism between man and computer. We must look at this with great concern, because it will create a new group of problems.

We are powerless against nature. We must be careful and respect her because we are not her master. There is only one Lord, and that is our God. We are not masters, neither are we conquers. We have to love and respect nature because it is really our home.

Works cited

The Holy Bible. New International Version.

Conradie, Ernst. "The Church and the Environment: Seven Stations towards the Sanctification of the Whole Earth." *Scriptura* 107, 2011, pp. 156-170.

Cook, John; Oreskes, Naomi; Doran, Peter; Anderegg, William; Verheggen, Bart; Maibach, Ed; Carlton, J. Stuart; Lewandowsky, Stephan; Skuce, Andrew; Green, Sarah; Nuccitelli, Dana; Jacobs, Peter; Richardson, Mark; Winkler, Bärbel; Painting, Rob; Rice, Ken. "Consensus on Consensus: A Synthesis of Consensus Estimates on Human-caused Global Warming". *Environmental Research Letters* 11, 2016, 048002. (referred to as Cook et al.) doi:10.1088/1748-9326/11/4/048002

Diffenbaugh, Noah; Burke, Marshall. "Global Warming has Increased Global Economic Inequality." *Proceedings of the National Academy of Sciences of the United States of America* 116 (20), 2019, pp. 9808-9813. www.pnas.org/cgi/doi/10.1073/pnas.1816020116

Falkner, Robert. "Global Environmentalism and the Greening of International Society." *International Affairs* 88 (3) 2012, pp. 503-522.

Foster, John Bellamy. "Marxism and Ecology: Common Fonts of a Great Transition." *The Jus Semper Global Alliance*, February 2020.

Pope Francis. Laudato si. (Encyclical letter). 24 May 2015 https://www.vatican.va/content/francesco/en/encyclicals/documents/papa-francesco_20150524_enciclica-laudato-si.html#_ftn11

Hegerl, Gabriele; Zwiers, Francis; Braconnot, Pascale; Gillett, Nathan; Luo, Yong; Marengo Orsini, Jose; Nicholls, Neville; Penner, Joyce; Stott, Peter A. "Understanding and Attributing Climate Change." Susan Solomon, Dahe Qin, Martin Manning, Zhenlin Chen, Melinda Marquis, Kristen Averyt, Melinda Tignor and Henry LeRoy Miller (eds.). *Climate Change 2007: The Physical Science Basis. Contribution of Working Group I to the Fourth Assessment Report of the Intergovernmental Panel on Climate Change*. Cambridge University Press, Cambridge, United Kingdom and New York, USA, 2007, pp. 663–745. (referred to as Hegerl et al.)

Hitzhusen, Gregory. "Judeo-Christian Theology and the Environment: Moving beyond Scepticism to New Sources for Environmental Education in the United States." *Environmental Education Research* 13 (1), February 2007, pp. 55–74.

King, David. "Climate Change Science: Adapt, Mitigate, or Ignore?" *Science* 303, 2004, pp. 176-8. https://science.sciencemag.org/content/303/5655/176/tab-pdf

Kurylo, Bohdana. "The Role of Chernobyl in the Breakdown of the USSR." *Armstrong Undergraduate Journal of History*, vol. 6 (1), 2016, Article 5, pp. 55- 66. DOI: 10.20429/aujh.2016.060105

Matzke, Jason P. "Human as 'Part and Parcel of Nature': Thoreau's Contribution to Environmentalist Ethics." *Ethics in Progress* 5 (2), 2014, pp. 170-186. doi: 10.14746/eip.2014.2.12

McNeill, J.R. "Observations on the Nature and Culture of Environmental History." *History and Theory* 42 (4), 2003, pp. 5-43.

Merchant, Nomaan. "Power Failure: How a Winter Storm Pushed Texas into Crisis". AP News, 21 February 2021. https://apnews.com/article/houston-football-storms-coronavirus-pandemic-hurricanes-5fd491ed5bfd9aa0ae08426c6078539e

Padua, Jose Augusto. "The Theoretical Foundations of Environment History." *Estudos avançados* 24 (68), 2010, pp. 81-101.

Paterson, Norman. "Global Warming: A Critique of the Anthropogenic Model and its Consequences." *Geoscience Canada*, 38 (1), 2011, pp. 41–48.

Pope Paul VI. Octogesima adveniens. (Apostolic letter.) 14 May 1971. https://www.vatican.va/content/paul-vi/en/apost_letters/documents/hf_pvi_apl_19710514_octogesima-adveniens.html

Pimentel, David; Herz, Megan; Glickstein, Michele; Zimmerman, Matthew; Allen, Richard; Becker, Katrina; Evans, Jeff; Hussain, Benita; Sarsfeld, Ryan; Grosfeld, Anat; Seidel, Thomas. "Renewable Energy: Current and Potential Issues." *BioScience* 52 (12) 2002, pp. 1111-1120. (referred to as Pimentel et al.)

Plested, James. "Capitalist Roots of the Environment Crisis." *Climate and Capitalism*, 18 February 2020. https://climateandcapitalism.com/2020/02/18/capitalist-roots-environment-crisis/

Rosen, Amanda. "The Wrong Solution at the Right Time: The Failure of the Kyoto Protocol on Climate Change." *Politics & Policy* 43 (1), 2015, pp. 30-58.

Shellenberger, Michael. "Why Apocalyptic Claims about Climate Change are Wrong." *Forbes*, 25 November 2019.

https://www.forbes.com/sites/michaelshellenberger/2019/11/25/why-everything-they-say-about-climate-change-is-wrong/?sh=3df90dd412d6

Skolimowski, Henryk. "For the Record: On the Origin of Eco-Philosophy." *The Trumpeter* http://trumpeter.athabascau.ca/index.php/trumpet/article/download/511/866?inline

Smith, Richard. "The Chinese Communist Party is an Environmental Catastrophe." *Foreign Policy*, 27 July 2020 https://foreignpolicy.com/2020/07/27/chinese-communist-party-environment-co2/

Stott, Peter; Stone, D.A.; Allen, M.R. "Human Contribution to the European Heatwave in 2003". *Nature* 432, December 2004, pp. 610- 614.

Turnock, David. "Environmental Problems and Policies in East Central Europe: A Changing Agenda." *GeoJournal*, Vol. 55 (2/4), 2001, pp. 485-505.

United Nations. The 2030 Agenda for Sustainable Development. (referred to as UN) https://sustainabledevelopment.un.org/content/documents/21252030%20Agenda %20for %20Sustainable%20Development%20web.pdf

Vaughan, David; Marshall, Gareth; Connolley, William; Parkinson, Claire; Mulvaney, Robert; Hodgson, Dominic; King, John C.; Pudsey, Carol; Turner, Johh. „Recent Rapid Regional Climate Warming on the Antarctic Peninsula". *Climatic Change* 60, 2003, pp. 243–274. (referred to as Vaughan et al.)

Waqainabete, Jeremaia. "Christian Environmentalism: An Ecotheological Approach to Earth Keeping." WWF Pacific, 2018. Part of the Sustainable Seafood project of the WWF.

https://wwf.panda.org/wwf_news/?335270/Christian-Environmentalism--An-Ecotheological-Approach-to-Earth-Keeping

www.ingramcontent.com/pod-product-compliance
Lightning Source LLC
LaVergne TN
LVHW082246150826
845677LV00009B/1544

* 9 7 9 8 8 6 9 1 7 9 9 4 4 *